Building Your
Child's Character
from the Inside Out

Building Your Child's Character from the Inside Out

Dr. Kay Kuzma

LIFEJOURNEY
BOOKS

DAVID C. COOK PUBLISHING CO.
Elgin, Illinois ❖ *Weston, Ontario*

LifeJourney Books™ is an imprint of David C. Cook Publishing Co.
David C. Cook Publishing Co., Elgin, Illinois 60120
David C. Cook Publishing Co., Weston, Ontario
Nova Distribution Ltd., Newton Abbot, England

BUILDING YOUR CHILD'S CHARACTER
FROM THE INSIDE OUT
©1988 by Kay Kuzma

Scripture quotations are from The Holy Bible, New King James Version, © 1982, 1985 Thomas Nelson, Inc. Used by permission.

Edited by Joan Guest
Cover design by Ad/Plus, Ltd.

First Paperback Printing, 1992
Printed in the United States of America
96 95 94 93 92 5 4 3 2 1

Kuzma, Kay
    Building Your Child's Character from the Inside Out
    1. Child rearing—Religious aspects—Christianity. 2. Child rearing—United States. I. Title.
    HQ769.3.K89 1988   649.1   88-8382

    ISBN 0-78140-936-5

ACKNOWLEDGMENTS

The book is finished! I sigh and lean back in my chair. "It is finished!" Then I glance out the window and see Kari and Kevin with their hair blowing in the wind and their backs bent to the task of weeding "my" rose garden. I could have never finished this book if it hadn't been for the kids.

Thanks . . .

. . . to my husband, Jan. He's still reading the final draft of this manuscript—putting on the finishing touches. This is his book, too. For almost twenty years, Jan and I have been in a building partnership—building our children's characters. This book is his philosophy, his stories, and his ideas, as much as mine. I admire Jan's strength of character. I have admired him from the first time we met when, while dressed in a suit and tie, he offered to add oil to his sister's car at the airport parking lot before flying back to Michigan. I was impressed with his thoughtfulness. I had never seen such a considerate brother—and I determined to get to know this guy better! I haven't been disappointed. Yes, Jan deserves the credit for this book.

. . . to my mother, Irene Humpal, who has a special love for all her children—and her grandchildren. Mom really was responsible for shaping my character. She wasn't always easy on me—but she was right! For everything I am today, I give her the credit. This book is my Mother's Day gift to her!

. . . to my thoughtful critic, Raylene Phillips, whose vision helped shape the book, and to Marijane Wallack and Edie

Westphal who helped me with the editing.

To all the above, thanks so much.

I have so much for which to be thankful—for family, friends and coworkers; for a lovely home and a weeded backyard; for book publishers and editors; for a support team that makes it possible for me to produce the daily syndicated "Parent Scene" radio program and television series; and . . . for each one of you who has listened to or read my words and have encouraged me with, "We're raising our kids by the Kuzma method, and they are such neat kids." God has blessed me abundantly. He has supplied all my needs. To Him be the glory.

DEDICATION

To Marion Poos . . .
one of the most beautiful characters I've met;
the sunshine and courage of Loma Linda.

CONTENTS

Chapter 1:   Introduction 1

Section I: Inside-Out Character
Chapter 2:   Inside-Out Character in
              an Upside-Down World 7
Chapter 3:   Character from the Inside Out................13
Chapter 4:   The IN-Factors.......................................19
Chapter 5:   Applying the In-Factors
              to Your Child's Life 25
Chapter 6:   Choosing Right from Wrong...................41
Chapter 7:   Peer-Pressure Proofing Your Child.........51
Chapter 8:   Helping Your Child to Know God............65

Section II: Concepts of Character for Kids
Chapter 9:   Having Treasure in Heaven 81
Chapter 10:   Worth the Effort....................................89
Chapter 11:   Character: God's Way 97

*Section III: Building Character
During the Growing Years*
Chapter 12:   Pregnancy and the First Year.................111
Chapter 13:   Toddler Years: One to Three.................121
Chapter 14:   Preschooler Years: Three to Six 131
Chapter 15:   Early School Years: Six to Nine.............145

Chapter 16: Later School Years:
             Nine to Twelve..155
Chapter 17: Teen Years...165

             Section IV: A Plan for
             Character Building
Chapter 18: Selecting Character Traits........................187
Chapter 19: Tools for Building Character....................197
Chapter 20: The Greatest Resource 211

             Epilogue
Appendix A: A Sample Plan for Developing
             Character Traits..227

Chapter 1
INTRODUCTION

This book was born with agony . . . and much prayer. How could I portray to parents the supreme importance of developing their child's character? I was tempted to give up. How could I make the most difficult subject in the world simple enough for all? It's too big! Character is so complex and encompassing.

I sat, as if in front of a giant puzzle, with hundreds of pieces spread before me. How could I put it all together? I can tell parents how to get their kids to behave, but right behavior is only a piece of the puzzle, and a little piece at that. Character includes thoughts, feelings, desires, and motives. It is words, looks, actions. Character is the outward reflection of the spiritual condition of the heart and mind. It's moving from a selfish nature, which we're all born with, to a Christlike nature. It's a lifelong process.

Plus, character building is a paradox. It's the most challenging task a child will ever have to face—daily overcoming that selfish nature. But it's not a work of "works"! In other words, just being good is not enough. It's a work of God: a stamp of His character on your child's individual personality and body structure.

Was I ready for the task? When is it "safe" to step out and share almost twenty years of experience? My own character is still under construction. And my family? We're certainly not perfect! But Jan and I wish you could meet our kids. Kim greets life with a smile and a warm embrace. Gifted in leadership she's eager to accept the challenge to be what God wants her to be and do what He wants her to do. Kari is our bubbly, enthusiastic charmer, who has a deep sensitivity to people—and a heart to help. In high school she's played on every varsity sports team and has a dream—the triathlon!

Meeting Kevin will warm your heart and if you want to see his eyes sparkle just mention surfing. He tackles his world with creativity and is the joy and challenge of our lives.

Most of all we are pleased that all three of our kids have a meaningful relationship with the Lord. We thank the Lord daily for the fruit that we see in our children's lives. Jan and I have only planted the seeds. The truth is that as much as parents plan, program, pray, and plead, they don't have full control of their child's character. At any point the child can say no to their influence and instruction. Daily our children are choosing for themselves whether or not to follow the Holy Spirit's direction for their lives—and whether or not to open the door of their hearts all the way, with no reservations, to their Savior, Jesus Christ.

Then why should I challenge parents to devote time and energy to molding and fashioning the foundation for their child's character? Why should I struggle to give parents a practical character-building guide that may make their job easier?

Why? Because a child's spiritual character will be molded—and molded early. It will either be molded by Christian parents or it will be molded by the world. Childhood is the critical window to a person's development of personality and soul. The baby and toddler is most open to your influence and instruction. By three years of age the child's basic personality has been established. By five, a child's brain is almost adult size, with over half of its capacity already in place. By seven, the child is pretty much a miniature of what he will be at maturity, and the window of opportunity to influence his character is less wide.

During these first seven years, the foundation for a child's character is most easily built. Changes can be made later, but with each passing year it becomes more difficult. That's why I feel this sense of urgency to inspire parents to meet the challenge NOW, regardless of a child's age. So no matter whether your child is three or ten or thirteen, remember that parental influence is greater today than tomorrow!

You are the owner of an orchard. You prepare the soil. You plant the tree. You nurture; you water; you shape and prune. You know your orchard—every tree is different. Some grow straight and tall and naturally open their branches to the sun. Other trees need support. As children begin to bend to the elements, they need you to train them: to straighten their trunks, to prune damaging growth, to spread their branches. But, with each passing year, the trunk gets more set; the branches more firm. The type of care the orchard will require in the future, and its productivity, will depend on the type of care you are willing to provide when the trees are young. You are the owner of an orchard . . . .

With a feeling of inadequacy I have labored over these pages, trying to make a complex subject just as clear and practical as I could, so you can be the best grower you can be. This is a book that will, I hope, be read by husbands and wives before their baby is born and then used as a reference throughout the growing years. It's never too late to begin the character-building process, so even if your child is into her teens, you'll find significant help.

My goal is to encourage you to develop your own character-building plan. To help you do this, I have given you specific guidelines for the different age levels and suggestions on how to introduce complex character concepts to kids. Plus, I have developed a sample plan for building character traits that you can adapt to any child's interest or age.

Please, use this guide with prayer and fasting. You'll need Spirit-directed wisdom to fashion a character-building program that will meet your child's needs.

My prayer is that your child will be open to your inspired influence, will accept your instruction, and will choose to develop a pure, spiritually sensitive, Christlike character—one that will be apparent to others as coming "from the inside out."

INSIDE-OUT CHARACTER

*F*ashioning and molding the spiritual character of your child is the most significant work
you can do, so your training for this task must
be not only comprehensive, but practical. If, in
your eagerness to get into this exciting subject,
you have neglected to read the introduction,
don't read further. It will give you an important foundation for the following material.

Now you are ready to delve into the meaning of character. Do you understand what character really is? When and how is it best
developed? What is the type of environment
that allows optimal development? What are the
key factors that you must use to be a successful
character builder? In this section, I will introduce you to the inside-out concept of character
and provide you with the basic information
that you will need to be the character builder
that God calls every parent to be.

Chapter 2
INSIDE-OUT CHARACTER
IN AN
UPSIDE-DOWN WORLD

I wasn't paying much attention. The TV was on in the other room so I didn't hear all the story, but it was something about this fellow who had a pet rock. It sat on his desk for weeks, months . . . it may have been years. Just a plain old ordinary rock.

Then one day someone noticed the rock, picked it up, examined it and recognized its potential. A rare find. A treasure that when cut and polished by caring hands would be worth millions.

At the mention of the extraordinary turn of events, I became interested and ran to the TV set just in time to see the stone being polished. The inside beauty, with its shape and rich blue color, was starting to appear. The pet rock was in the process of becoming a stunning, multiple-karat gem!

As I reflected on the story, I wondered how many of our children are like that pet rock. We live with them; we've grown accustomed to their ways but are oblivious of their true value. They can probably make it through life as they are—just plain old pet rocks! But with some cutting and polishing by caring hands, their true potential can emerge. No matter what his or her exterior may look like, with a "polished" spiritual character every child can accomplish a noble work for God by blessing humanity. Your child can make a real difference in the confused world today!

The importance of actively building a child's character was made clear to me when I was miles above this earth. "We have reached our cruising altitude of 35,000 feet," the pilot's voice came crackling over the intercom. "But as you've noticed, it's a little choppy up here. We're doing everything we can to make your ride as comfortable as possible, but . . . ." I tightened my seat belt. No longer could I concentrate on my book, so I put it down, dug my fingernails into the armrests and turned to my seatmate. "I hate turbulence," I muttered as the plane bounced through the air. My seat mate laughed. We began to chat, and our minds focused on a more absorbing topic.

He was an administrator of a large juvenile detention facility with more than nine hundred incarcerated kids. In the course of our conversation I learned that this facility, although one of the best, had only a forty percent success rate in preparing the kids to fit into society without having them return at some future date.

When I probed for an answer to why the majority of the kids ended up back in jail, he responded, "These kids have never heard of integrity. Their value systems are confused —upside down—and we have to lay a foundation for a new way of thinking. For example, take the work ethic. These kids have never heard of things like an honest day's work for a day's pay. Instead, they feel that you only go to work to get by with as little as you can. What you do doesn't matter as long as you put in the time, and the more you can rip off your employer— the smarter you are.

"Such confused values, however, only set them up to fail in the future," he added. "We've got to teach these kids, from the inside out, a whole new set of values. And it's difficult to do what needs to be done so late in life—and in such a short period of time. If they could have a more supportive family or peer group when they return to society, it would make a real difference."

I was troubled with what he said. Yet I knew that the philosophy and way of life of many people today is opposite to God's way. For example, the Bible says: "Freely you have received, freely give; the least shall be the most; the last shall be first; love your enemies; be kind to those who hate you; pray for those who do terrible things to you; lend without expecting repayment; the humble shall see God; healing comes through brokenness; finding yourself comes through losing yourself; turn the other cheek, and new life springs from giving up the old."

Now, contrast God's way with the confused, upside-down way of the world. The world says: "Get what you can while the gettin's good; you've got to look out for #1; you can achieve whatever you want—just go for it and don't let anything or anybody stop you; treat people as they deserve to be treated; go after what you've got coming; don't let anyone trample on your rights; you can heal yourself with the right attitude; win through intimidation, find yourself through self-actualization and psychotherapy; don't bury the past—analyze it . . ." and on and on.

The inside, dominant motivating force for the worldly person today is self-gratification, winning by whatever means possible, acting dishonest as long as you don't get caught, solving problems with violence, performing questionable acts as long as it feels good, and having little respect for authority. We are a generation grown spiritually indifferent—allowing the world to shape our internal values.

There is a character crisis in our culture. Where are the Honest Abes or the Trumans who have the strength of character to say, "The buck stops here"? Instead, we have Watergates, Contra Affairs, and TV evangelists who repent only when they get caught.

It's easy to blame the immorality of screen artists or the drug abuse of rock stars for negatively influencing the character of our young people today. However, a careful assessment of the problem would likely point to the negative experiences within the home during the child's early years as the imperfect foundation for godly character development.

An effective way to solve this crisis is with a plan that starts within your own heart and home, and starts now! Postponement will only make the task more difficult. Halfhearted resolve will never do it. Outside pressures are very strong. Building your child's character must become your all-consuming passion. But it can't be done effectively unless you are working daily on your own character development—a task that is equally challenging!

How can our children develop godly characters in a society that doesn't know the meaning of integrity? Disciplining for good behavior isn't enough. Somehow we have to instill integrity, which by definition is the quality or state of being of sound moral principle; uprightness, honesty, and sincerity; in perfect condition; complete. We must develop those fundamental, biblical principles that will help them develop distinctive characters in spite of growing up among corrupting influences.

True character development must begin on the inside with

correct motives, unselfish desires, and pure thoughts that come as a result of having a close relationship with God. When kids are spiritually healthy, we don't have to worry about them catching society's "colds"!

Parents want good kids, but they too often expect the church to give them spiritual instruction, the school to motivate them to learn, Little League to inspire fair play, and the local place of business to teach them how to work. Every experience in a child's life will help shape his attitudes and desires. But you, Mom and Dad, must accept the responsibility for being the planter and gardener, commissioned by the Master to bring about the realization of the Designer's blueprint.

You must assume the responsibility for developing your child's character, and with the Master Designer's help, nurture it, inspire it, and polish it until your child's character is everything God intended it to be—Christlike and beautiful "from the inside out." That's a real treasure in this confused, upside-down world.

Chapter 3
CHARACTER FROM THE INSIDE OUT

What type of person would you like your child to become? He or she probably will not achieve the best unless you plan to "cut" the objectionable traits and nurture or "polish" the less visible, but positive ones. That will make it possible for your child to have a vibrant, indomitable character.

I'd like you to meet Marion. Her perspective on life might modify your dream of what you want your child to be.

I met her eight years ago—a vivacious, 23-year-old student, with long auburn hair, a winsome smile, and a lilt in her step as she walked down the halls of the School of Public Health where I taught. Marion was a friend to everyone.

I remember the first little note: a verse that Marion wrote to my husband thanking him, her biostatistics professor, for his interest in students. What a thoughtful gesture. But I soon learned that this wasn't an isolated incident. Now, I, too, have received my share of little notes. Original verse, quaint drawings, a word of appreciation, and always the red paper hearts falling from the envelope. I've seen a rose, swaddled in dainty baby's breath, on a secretary's desk. "How beautiful!"

"Marion gave it to me."

This is life to Marion—reaching out to others with love and creativity. She is something special.

I didn't realize how special, however, until the word spread—"Marion has cancer!" The child of an innocent mother who took DES to prevent a miscarriage, Marion has been through what most of us would consider a living hell. Her first bout with cancer actually came before her first birthday, but the disease didn't return again until her twenty-fourth year. Surgery, chemotherapy, radiation. Drugs, more drugs, and drugs to counteract the effect of drugs. Lupus, kidney and liver malfunction, nausea, a disturbed sense of balance, a body that refused to manufacture white blood cells to ward off infections, seizures, loss of hair, and finally an automobile accident that broke most of the bones on the right side of her body and gave her what many people thought was a one-way ticket to the Intensive Care Unit.

But Marion defied the odds, and a couple of months later went home; not to a convalescent home where she could be cared for, but to her own apartment where she could begin the torturous process of rehabilitation, with bones that refused to heal, pain that refused to subside, and a will that refused to give up. The emergency phone number became her salvation and ICU her repeated residence. Throughout this terrible ordeal, her spirit of determination, although at times wavering, never died even though her leg had to be amputated. She had a goal to finish her doctorate in Public Health and on the way to befriend others with little notes like:

Roses are red,
The sky's getting blue,
The week's going to be great,
And I love you.

Most of us would have been tempted to follow Job's friend's advice to "curse God and die." But not Marion. Instead

14

of wilting under bodily persecution, she bloomed. During the early hours before dawn when pain became so intense that sleep was a stranger, Marion would jot down her feelings. For example, on one occasion she wrote:

"To wish for our own death before the disease forces it, is a tragedy. Death will come, because everything that lives must die. Even stars die. Life is now . . . . Take the dares, the double dares, and try."

"Anxiety is the unwillingness to play, even when you know the odds are for you. Courage is the willingness to play, even when you know the odds are against you."

" 'Where there's a will, there's a way,' isn't true. But it is true that where there is no will, there is no way."

Marion knows how to play the game of life. Marion has a will—a strength of character—that won't give up. One time I asked, "Marion, you have such a beautiful character, to what do you contribute it?"

She laughed, and with that characteristic lilt, responded, "I don't see myself that way. I think I'm a pain in the neck!" Then on a more serious note she continued, "When it comes down to the bottom line, it has to be God. He made me and He's such an artist. So creative. He made me in His image. He gave me life. That makes me responsible for reflecting His image with my life and my creativity. His gift of life and creativity are expressions of love for me, and I must pass them on. That's why I have a passion for living. It's just that simple. I love to love—to the best of my ability."

Then she reflected, "I have a strong sense of how sad God must be when something tragic happens, like when He looks down and sees me with my broken body, because He doesn't want it to be like this. But in spite of it all, He has given me laughter over things that are so pitiful and painful that they aren't really funny—and God's design for healing is working. ('A merry heart does good, like medicine' Proverbs 17:22.) It's waking up the healing chemicals in my brain; it's working on my bone marrow—I'm now making white blood cells. Let's face it, it's hard work. But most of all, it's grace!"

When I think of a person with an unconquerable character, I think of Marion. She isn't perfect, but I sure admire her. When you think of a person with strength of character, who comes to your mind? A person with the ability to think clearly and make good decisions? Someone with a good reputation? A refined or self-confident person? Someone who holds a high and responsible position? A loyal church member? An obedient child? These are all wonderful characteristics, but character is more than what is portrayed by them. These qualities only convey the exterior, or outside manifestation, of character.

Trying to understand character is a little like trying to understand a car. It would be rather simple if the accelerator, brakes, and steering wheel were all that was needed to make it function, but these are only the most obvious parts that put the car in motion. There are the wheels, the electrical system and battery, the starter, motor, lights, fuel, and, of course, the body style, color, sound, and smell that help to make a Buick a Buick and a Ford a Ford! It is rather difficult to say which part is the most important since they all are so interrelated.

And so it is with character. It's not just one thing.

True character—character that really makes a difference when the chips are down, as in Marion's case, manifests itself from the inside out. It's the wholeness of one's thoughts, desires, motives, feelings, speech, behavior, habits, and the choices one makes. Character is not just doing all the right things. It's thinking the right thoughts; it's having the right motives; it's feeling the right feelings; it's making the right choices. It's the wholeness of a person's inward thinking and outward behavior. It is the quality of the soul as it is revealed in conduct. But most of all, as Marion said, "It's grace." It's God's power working from the inside out.

Men and women throughout history have tried to make themselves look good to others. In Jesus' day it was the scribes and Pharisees who followed the letter of the law and, therefore, thought they were better than others. But Jesus clearly stated that "unless your righteousness exceeds that of the scribes and Pharisees, you will never enter the kingdom of heaven" (Matthew 5:20, RSV).

Just teaching a child to do the right thing is not enough. Jesus clarified what keeping the commandments really meant when He included feelings, thoughts, and words, as well as actions, as ways in which the commandments could be broken.

For example: He said, "You have heard that it was said to men of old, 'You shall not kill; and whoever kills shall be liable to judgment.' But I say to you that every one who is angry with his brother shall be liable to judgment; whoever insults his brother shall be liable to the council, and whoever says, 'You fool!' shall be liable to the hell of fire" (Matthew 5:21, 22, RSV). Suddenly the commandment, "You shall not kill," steps on my toes. I've been guilty of getting angry; my words have sometimes been insulting, and the thought, "You fool," has at times passed silently across my lips! None of us is perfect. We must continue to grow toward Christlikeness and help our children to do the same!

To be successful inside-out character builders, we must have a goal. The goal must be for more than just good behavior. I want my children to have valiant characters like Marion's—that regardless of unfortunate circumstances or tremendous temptations, can continue to radiate God's love and remain loyal to Him. I want them to develop integrity—to do what is right even if no one is watching, or even if the majority is not doing it, or even when the consequences are negative. I want them to be unselfish. I would like them to exhibit wholesome character traits. I pray they will do noble tasks for God and be an encouragement to humanity by radiating a love for Jesus, their Savior. I have a dream that their lives will make a difference in this world. My goal is for inside-out character, and I hope that you will adopt this goal for your children as well.

Chapter 4
THE IN-FACTORS

A child's character development shouldn't be left to chance. A goal is not enough. You also need a plan for reaching that goal. In order to be successful, your character-training plan must include three essential factors, all of which begin with IN: INfluence, INformation, and INternal control. I call them the IN-factors.

Marv Marinovich was a dad who believed that a child's development shouldn't be left to chance—at least not his physical development. The story of this father's dedication to his son's athletic excellence is astounding. I hope it might jar us character-building parents out of our lethargy and inspire us to develop a training plan that will make us as successful in developing character as Todd's dad was in developing athletic ability.

Marv's experience playing and coaching football made him realize that the days of the "born" football hero were over. Top athletes are trained athletes. And that's what he wanted for his son, Todd. So, before Todd's birth, Marv set up a plan—a long-term training program for his child. As part of the plan, Marv's wife ate only natural foods and had no extra salt or sugar and no alcohol or tobacco during her pregnancy. She wanted to ensure the best prenatal influences on Todd's development. After Todd was born, his dad started doing stretching and flexing exercises with him while Mom fed him mother's milk and fresh-cooked, strained vegetables. Throughout the growing years Todd's diet was carefully monitored, his folks even packed him healthful lunches when he attended parties where junk foods were served.

When Todd was still a baby he started playing with balls: big balls, weighted balls, small balls. Later Marv showed Todd how to throw with either hand and to kick with either leg, to walk on a balance beam, and run. To celebrate his fourth birthday, Todd ran four miles. That's not an easy task at any age! By age six, Todd had tried gymnastics and ballet and was enrolled in baseball and basketball leagues. In addition, Todd and Marv did a daily workout which included special exercises and practicing whatever sport was in season.

The result of all this training? Todd has been called by some the "perfect athlete." His first year in high school he became the starting quarterback for the varsity squad. He has been racking up records ever since, including "Offensive Player of the Year" for the high school ALL-USA Football Team. In 1988 he held the national high school record with 9,149 passing yards. His high school coach said that Todd didn't have a single weakness (which is probably why university football recruiters beat a path to his door). He also said, "Ask a lot of kids who are big in sports about themselves, and it's all, 'I did this, I did that.' I, me, mine. You gotta drag that stuff out of Todd. He's got the littlest head of any athlete I've ever met." From all appearances, Todd seems to be a normal, happy, socially secure, well-adjusted teen.

Todd's story is just beginning. I have no idea how the final chapters of his life might read, but I'm impressed with his accomplishments so far. I'm not recommending that every mom and dad put their child on an athletic training schedule at birth—and anyway, there is no scientific evidence that kicking a ball at age one produces a punter at age twenty. But something made a difference in Todd's life. What was it?

I believe the difference was that Todd's dad had a plan. Here's what Marv said: "I wanted the best possible environment for him to develop in. I believe there is no limit to potential ability—the genetic limits are overrated. The secret is to start early with a life-style and commitment that are designed with purpose. For some fathers, nothing is more important than their jobs or the stock market. For me, it was my two kids. Nothing mattered more.

"I always made time for Todd. I never missed a game or a practice session. I provided discipline, healthy foods, measurable goals, a desire to improve, and positive support. I didn't program him; I only surrounded him with an excellent environment."

Just as Marv Marinovich had a training plan for Todd, we must have training plans for our children. It doesn't matter whether we are training them for athletic excellence or good character. To be successful, we must use the same principles that made Marv's plan succeed.

We must apply the three essential IN-factors: INfluence, INformation, and INternal control. A child's character is developing continually, influenced by people or events in his life, the information he receives, and his growing internal control. There is no 100 percent guarantee for the outcome of character development, but with a suitable training plan you can certainly increase your odds for success.

Let's go back to Todd's story and see how his dad used these factors to make his training plan work.

INfluence

Marv Marinovich had a tremendous influence on his son's life. Not only was he an example, but Todd's training and development were so important that he didn't allow anyone else to supervise them. The time he invested in Todd has paid off. He has passed onto Todd his vision, his persistence, and his willpower to deny self-gratification for the ultimate goal of excellence. Marv also brought other influential people into Todd's life to provide the information Todd needed to help him reach his goal. This brings us to the second factor.

INformation

Marv Marinovich hired specialists to coach Todd. For example, one coach worked on increasing Todd's speed and precision. Someone else improved his overall strategy for passing. A third worked on the coordination of body movements, while another analyzed how the football came off Todd's fingers. A physician helped Todd improve his hand-eye coordination and peripheral vision, a nutritionist made sure Todd ate the right diet, and another specialist designed protective equipment for him to wear. And this is only a partial list of all those who have coached Todd!

But what if Todd didn't accept the advice of his father and the specialists? This brings us to the final, and most important, IN-factor.

INternal Control

As important as influence and information are for a child's development, both must take a backseat to internal control. Without internal control, or self-discipline, the others are meaningless. In other words, at any time Todd was free to ignore the positive influences around him or reject the information that was given to him. He could say, as so many teens do, "I don't care what you tell me. I know best, and I'm going to do it my way." If Todd would have chosen to do this, there really wouldn't be much that his father could do. That's why internal control is the key to making the best use of influence and information.

Many kids would have rebelled under the extreme pressure that Todd experienced. Why didn't Todd? There must have been the right combination of encouragement and motivation from his dad. Todd knew that his father was devoted to him. Somehow the rapport between father and son was strong enough to link the two of them together in achieving their goal.

Isn't it interesting how much time and effort parents will spend on developing their children's skills and abilities —whether it's music, academics, or football—and how little time is spent on the more important aspects of life, like a child's character? I'm not saying that time spent making a child into a top-rate quarterback isn't also building character. It's just that character development is not the focus. I wonder what spiritual giants we would have today if parents would devote the same amount of time planning and implementing a training plan for their children's character as Marv Marinovich did to develop athletic excellence in Todd?

Chapter 5
APPLYING IN-FACTORS
TO YOUR CHILD'S LIFE

You have a goal: a child with a spiritually based inside-out character. You have the essential ingredients that you must use in your training plan: influence, information, and internal control. Now you need a coach—a teacher. However, in the area of character development you don't have a choice. You are your child's first and most influential teacher whether you want to be or not! But before you can initiate your specific plan to reach your goal, you must understand how to apply the IN-factors in the character-building process.

Using INfluence

In a restaurant in Honolulu, Jan and I were enjoying the entertainment provided by a Hawaiian trio. Each member was playing a ukulele. By far the most agile was the baritone uke player. His fingers raced over the strings. But the most fascinating thing was that he was playing his ukulele backwards—with his left hand strumming! How could anyone play an instrument so well—backwards? Later he explained that when he was a little boy his grandmother used to play her ukulele for him as he would sit across from her. He learned to play by simply imitating her. He was her mirror image.

In a way our children are like mirror images of us. If we don't like what we see in our children, we should carefully examine ourselves, because chances are their behavior has been influenced by ours!

A vivid illustration of a negative parental influence is how alcoholism, suicide, abuse, and even divorce tend to run in families. It doesn't have to, but if children have witnessed these strong emotion-producing events as a way to deal with a problem, it becomes a more viable option for them to use in the future when confronted with a similar situation.

You may have difficulty relating to examples of severe dysfunctional behavior, such as alcoholism, suicide, or abuse, or even with the more common impact of divorce, but parental influence is so strong that even "little" faults, such as overeating, watching too much TV, and criticizing, can have an equally powerful effect. In fact, just a few minutes ago, I said, "Kevin, I want you to clean your closet."

My fifteen-year-old smiled a "chessy cat" grin and said, "Mom, I was just waiting for you to ask me that, because the other day I looked in your closet, and mine doesn't look much different." Now, what is a parent to do? I guess I'll just have to clean my closet!

I still remember the impact Sandy and Harry Chapin's song, "Cat's in the Cradle," had on me as a young, and overly busy mother. The song is about a son wanting his father to spend time with him. The father, however, is always too busy with other things. But, throughout the song, the child continues to say, "I'm gonna be like you, Dad, you know I'm gonna be like you." It's the message of the last verse that knocks one off one's feet. The father had retired and his son had moved away. Now the father is asking the son when he can come for a visit, and the son replies that he is too busy. The father then laments, "And as I hung up the phone, it occurred to me—he'd grown up just like me."

What kind of an influence does your mode of living and your personality have upon your child? It's quite likely that he will grow up to be very much like you!

This can have frightening results on your child if you lack self-esteem, or if you don't have control over some negative influence of your child's other parent. It is impossible to right all the wrongs that your child may have experienced in the past. What should you do if your child has already been influenced by such things as alcoholism, suicide, abuse, or inadequate parental love? Let's talk about specifics.

What if you lack self-esteem? Your perception of yourself has been influenced by many things, including the way your own parents have treated you throughout childhood and whether or not you have been able to live up to the expectations you have for yourself.

1. Evaluate carefully why you don't think much of yourself. Those things which you can't change, you must pray that God will help you to accept, similarly as God accepts you— just as you are. God designed you for a special work. Your looks, skills, personality, and spiritual gifts all go together to help you fulfill His purpose for your life. Your weaknesses may be the very things God can use so that you can better meet someone else's needs, but it's hard to believe this when you see yourself in a negative light. So, if you are feeling negative about yourself, pray that God will open your eyes and reveal to you the benefits of what you consider weaknesses.

2. Dwell on key Bible texts that indicate how valuable you are. Your value comes from God, not from what you look like or what you do! Here are a few texts to get you started:

   * God created you (Psalm 139:13-16).

   * God knew you and what you would become, before your birth (Jeremiah 1:5).

   * God even allowed the death of His Son in order to give you eternal life (John 3:16).

   * God is preparing a home in heaven for you (I John 3:16).

   * God calls you His child (I John 3:1).

   * God has inscribed your name on the palms of His hands (Isaiah 49:16).

   * God wants to cover your filthy-rag righteousness with His robe of righteousness (Isaiah 64:6).

3. Make a plan for yourself to consistently work on overcoming some of the things you can change. Maybe it's losing weight, or not losing your temper. Whatever it might be, set realistic, small goals and celebrate the achievements of these goals. See yourself in the process of becoming. Keep telling yourself that God isn't finished with you yet!

4. Begin focusing on your strengths. Do those things that you do well. Maybe you should make a list of the things you like about yourself. You may be surprised!

5. Are you a perfectionist? Perhaps your ideals and expectations for yourself are unrealistic. You may have a goal to be a perfect parent. If so, every time your child does something wrong you become discouraged and experience a sense of failure. Perfect parents and perfect kids don't

exist! You must change your unrealistic expectation.

6. If your children are old enough, you may want to discuss with them how you have felt about yourself in the past and how this may have affected the way you treated them. You will want to ask for their forgiveness if you have been abusive or neglectful. Then, reinforce to them how valuable they are to God, regardless of the mistakes you may have made as a parent. Your willingness to be open and honest will make a tremendous impression on them and will go a long way toward erasing the negative influence you might have had on them in the past.

7. Do some unexpected favor for someone who deserves your love. Reaching out to others often has the result of an overwhelming flow of appreciation and love back to the giver.

Only when we can feel good about ourselves will we be able to discharge effectively God's command to "Love our neighbor (including each of our family members) as we love ourselves." Experiencing love has a "magical" power to right more effectively those hurtful wrongs as nothing else can do.

What if you can't control some negative influence of the other parent?

This is sometimes a heartbreaker! There are no easy answers. You cannot be responsible for the behavior of another person, and yet because parental influence has a tremendous impact on character development, you may feel you must do something to protect your child. What you do will depend upon the age of your child, the negative influence of that behavior, and whether or not you are living with that person. If the child's other parent is exhibiting a behavior that may be abusive, either physically or verbally, you have a responsibility to protect your child by attempting to change that behavior, and if that doesn't work, going to court to get legal protection.

Putting your head in the sand, so to speak, and hoping that the abuse will go away, can be devastating to your child. Your child desperately needs relief from negative influence. Professional help might certainly be an avenue to consider.

What if one parent is living a deviant life-style? Perhaps he's into pot, pornography, or homosexuality, or maybe he's having an affair and he wants his child to spend time with him in the same household where all this is going on.

What if one parent is constantly downgrading a child, and you see your child begin to wilt under this onslaught of persecution?

What if one parent has turned against God and is openly rebellious, putting down your beliefs and your church and offering other activities during worship times. It's unfair to ask a small child to choose between the excitement of Disneyland and attending church.

If you find yourself in this position, here are some general guidelines:

1. Stand up for what you know is right. Your example is important. You may not control the influence of questionable entertainment and negative habits that your child is exposed to when he's with the other parent, but if you feel it's wrong, you don't have to be a part of it. Your consistency in maintaining reasonable standards will have an effect upon your child.

    Sometimes the rebellious parent is only making empty threats to provoke you, like wanting to take your child to a questionable movie, when you feel he should go to church with you. Don't fall into this trap. Keep cool, calm, and collected. Be truthful about how you feel the negative influence will affect your child. Give sound reasons. Say, "I cannot allow our child to be exposed to examples of immorality." You'll be surprised how many times you'll be able to negotiate a reasonable solution just by seeking to clarify your differences in a thoughtful manner with the other parent. Be willing to listen to the other parent. Remember, he or she has rights, too!

2. Disapprove of the behavior, but don't downgrade the other parent. Your child is genetically a part of both of you. That's a fact you can't change. When you criticize the other parent, the child's identity suffers. Say to your child something like, "I believe smoking is wrong because it is very unhealthy. But your daddy has developed a habit that is hard to break. We can pray that God will give him the power to stop."

3. Allow your child to talk of his feelings about these influences and discuss what he can do about them. Many times the child has more influence on a parent choosing to change than a spouse does! I know a number of parents who have responded positively to their child saying, "Daddy, why don't you stop smoking? I don't want you to die." Or, "Mommy, why don't you go to church with us? I want to live with you in heaven."

What if your child has already been influenced by past negative experiences—such as alcoholism, divorce, or abuse?

1. Make sure your child does not feel he was the cause of these things. He was not responsible for what happened. Take time to discuss this fact, because the irrational guilt he may feel is not conducive to healthy character development.

2. Help your child realize that just because there is a family background for such experiences, it is not necessary for them to occur again. A child can't choose his family, but a child can choose how he allows his family's past to influence his life. So, don't be discouraged if you can't correct a negative past experience for your child. Just be aware of the potentially strong influence it can have and protect your child by emphasizing that he has the ability to choose a better way. Help him learn positive ways to cope with it. He can choose, with the help of God, to make a negative into a positive. For example, he might be able to help another person in a similar situation, because his negative past has taught him to be more sensitive and understanding.

3. Emphasize the positive. In a way the old clichè, "Character is caught, not taught," has a lot of truth to it. Your positive role model can have a significant impact, especially with certain traits. For example, how do you teach a child to respect other cultures and to sacrifice to meet their needs? No song, story, or object lesson is going to have the impact your own personal behavior will have. My editor told me that she learned this trait by accompanying her mom as she tutored Black kids in an inner-city. And where did her mom acquire this willingness to serve? From her mother as she traveled back and forth to an Indian Reservation to help establish a library. Your influence is important. Make sure your child has an opportunity to be involved with you as you demonstrate important character traits in your own life. For more ideas on how you can be an important resource in your character-building plan for your children, see Chapter 18.

Influence is only one aspect of being a good character-building teacher. Another is that of sharing information.

Conveying INformation

You are your child's best source of information, especially during the early years. That's why I refer to parents as teachers. Since children learn better from teachers they respect than from those they fear, you must ask yourself how you can maintain your child's respect. Recall those teachers you respected and those who have had the greatest influence on your life. Chances are you will agree that the following list portrays the essential qualities of successful teachers. Adapting these qualities will help you to become an effective teacher as well.

1. Live by the same standards you hold for others. This means in your speech and in your actions, in the music you listen to, the movies you watch, and the things you eat. It's not easy being a good teacher, is it?

2. Demonstrate your unconditional acceptance by curbing your anger and criticism. You may say you love your child, but if you get angry and lash out with uncontrolled words and actions, or if you criticize, threaten, compare your child unfavorably with others, or make sarcastic comments about your child, he won't feel loved, and will tend to tune out your words of wisdom.

3. Own up to your own failures and mistakes, and be quick to apologize. Let your child see that you are human. Kids can't respect teachers who won't take responsibility for their own behavior, and who are always making excuses or blaming something, or someone else, for their mistakes. You don't have to always be right!

4. Play with your children; laugh; enjoy yourself. Be fun to be with. Never give your kids the idea that time spent with them is wasted. More character can be taught shooting baskets, than shooting off your mouth!

5. Make your lessons interesting. If you want to keep their attention and hold down the discipline problems while you are trying to teach them, make sure that your presentation of information is age-appropriate. Kids tune out boring lessons. Talk up to them—never down. But don't expect them to be little adults, either. Use a variety of techniques, and whatever you do, be creative. Sure, it takes a little more time—but chances are you will find the quality of your lessons will be in direct proportion to the amount of preparation you do.

6. Listen more than you talk. A good teacher is a good listener. Ask a thought-provoking question and wait for answers. Make it safe for kids to make comments. Accept their ideas by saying, "That's an interesting thought," rather than blurting, "That's a crazy idea!" Don't tag a moral onto every lesson. Let your children discuss what they have learned from what you have said. When children are actively involved in the learning situation, they will retain the information longer.

7. Reward for achievement. Be quick to notice when improvements have been made. Smile, wink, give them a hug, or in some way let them know that you are tuned in to them and appreciate their efforts. Encourage your children by offering incentives when it's appropriate, but don't foster competition by giving a prize to the "best." Make everyone a winner, no matter how minute the progress.

8. Say what you mean and mean what you say. Be consistent. Keep your promises. Follow through on imposing consequences. Don't be indifferent to hurtful behavior, whether it hurts the child, others, or things. Make your children think you have eyes in the back of your head. Don't be a pushover. Yet, at the same time, if you have been too tough, don't be afraid to admit it and work out a more just and reasonable solution. Keep involved.

9. Be an effective disciplinarian. Learn how to motivate, encourage and influence, rather than merely control. Trust your kids when it's appropriate. Allow them to grow toward independence. Don't be overly protective. If it really doesn't matter, allow your children to do things their own way, rather than having to do things your way. Disciple them. Learn how to lead.

10. Treat your children as if they are really "hot stuff"—something special. Children love to be special. Make them feel good by saying things like, "You do so many nice things, this paper isn't big enough for me to write them all down." "You really can play a mean game of tennis!" But be sure your praise is honest! If children receive enough positive strokes naturally from parents, they don't have to show off or beat others down for attention. Kids love to be with people whom they know think they are tops! You will find your task of teaching values more successful if you preteach. In other words, teach your children the importance of certain values and begin helping them clarify how they feel about certain issues before they get to the critical age when these will affect the decisions they make.

For example, when should you begin discussing the type of

person your daughter should marry? It's too late when she's head over heels in love with the character down the block. You start pointing out characteristics that make a good husband during the early years when she thinks she wants to grow up and marry Daddy. When you see a teen playing with small children, comment about how important it is to marry someone who likes children. Encourage your school-age son, as he visits the homes of his friends and finds out what other mothers are like, to begin making a list of characteristics he would like to have in a wife.

Choosing a spouse is just one area where preteaching is valuable. Other examples of critical areas that often cause problems as children grow are:

1. Types of entertainment.

2. Styles of dress.

3. Appropriate dating behavior.

If you start early enough, discussing these value-laden issues before your child is being pressured by society and peers, your information will be much more acceptable. Encourage your child to set high standards for behavior in these areas. The more he feels it is his value and not just Mom's or Dad's—the more he owns it—the stronger will be his resistance to wordly pressure.

Being an effective teacher is quite a challenge. Nevertheless, try to have fun and be encouraging in all situations.

Teaching INternal Control

Internal control is the most important factor in a child's character development. Parents can help the child become wise and strong in this area by making sure he realizes that he is responsible for his own life, by teaching him how to make good decisions, and by encouraging self-discipline.

As early as possible you should try to get across to your child that he is responsible for what he will be. You may be legally responsible for him until he's eighteen, but in reality, even during those preschool years, he is responsible for controlling his emotions, for what he does, and the habits he chooses to adopt. In fact, the earlier you can have him accept responsibility for the choices he will make, the better it will be for his character development. Your responsibility is to provide information and to influence him. Your child's responsibility is to choose to use what you offer. Here are some suggestions to make this philosophy practical:

1. Make sure your child understands that he is responsible for his own emotions and behavior. Daddy doesn't make him angry. He chooses to let Daddy's behavior aggravate him and make him angry. He could have chosen to ignore Daddy's behavior! Or, he could choose to accept Daddy just the way he is and not let his abrasive ways get under his skin. It's the child's choice, if he allows Daddy's behavior to ruin his day.

2. Don't let the child blame you when he has to suffer certain consequences. He could have chosen to obey.

3. Don't let your child excuse his own behavior because of something you have done in the past. Just because you came down on him pretty hard last time he lied, you are not responsible for his lying behavior. He chose to take his chances and tell another lie hoping that he wouldn't get caught.

4. Parental influence is strong—but it can be overcome if your child chooses to overcome it. If he heard you and your spouse yelling at each other, admit that yelling is not acceptable and tell him that your previous failure is no excuse for him to yell. He can choose to overcome bad habits, as well as undesirable inherited tendencies.

5. Don't overprotect your child from things that should be his responsibility. In other words, it's not your fault your child had to stay after school because he didn't get his homework done. Sure, you went shopping last night, but he chose to go along. He could have chosen to stay home and do his homework instead.

This philosophy may sound pretty severe. But if you continue to accept the responsibility for your child's decisions, he will also let you take the blame. He may still be blaming you when he is thirty and having trouble in his own marriage. "My folks never trained me how to budget my money; it's their fault I'm in financial difficulty." "If my folks had just spent more time with me, I'd have a better self-concept." "I never was allowed to watch TV, that's why I'm a TV junky today." These arguments aren't very convincing. They are excuses for a lack of self-discipline. Sure, we are molded by our folks, and because of the way they have raised us we may have some negative odds to overcome, but we ultimately make our own choices!

The earlier you allow your child to make decisions that are appropriate for him to make, and allow him to enjoy or suffer the resulting consequences, the better. Children need to have the freedom not only to succeed but also to fail. Many valuable lessons can be learned from failures as well. Good decision makers are generally experienced decision makers. When a child has the assurance that you will allow him to make certain decisions, he doesn't have to become rebellious in order to get his own way. Give him plenty of opportunities to use his own judgment while he is still under your care and protection, and you are in a position to give valuable instruction and counsel. (For more about teaching children to be responsible see my book, *A Hug and a Kiss and a Kick in the Pants,* Elgin, Ill: David C. Cook, 1987. Chapters 9, 14, 30, 31, and 32.)

Teaching a child to be self-disciplined is so important that I have included this character trait as a part of A Sample Plan for Character Development (see appendix A).

Chapter 6
CHOOSING RIGHT FROM WRONG

What would you do if...

...bags of money fell out of an armored truck, and the truck kept on going down the freeway?

...you found a wallet loaded with ten-and twenty-dollar bills and no one was around?

...you opened a briefcase that was filled with cash and no ID?

...a waitress had not picked up the tip from the previous customer?

The answer is simple, isn't it? You would return the money. You would do everything possible to find the rightful owner. Would you? Well, according to a recent article in *Time* magazine (Ezra Bowen, "Whatever Became of Honest Abe?" 4 April 1988, p. 68), that's not what most people would do. "Finders-keepers" seems to be the moral code that many adults are living by today. The article centers around incidents when money was lost off armored vehicles, most of which was never returned. And even when it is, the honest Abe is not always applauded—even by his parents. For example, when one man returned $57,000 he said his mother was proud of him, but his father said, "I thought I raised you better than that!"

God's moral code is clear: "Thou shalt not steal." And yet

many rationalize dishonest behavior. "Society owes it to me because of the way I've been treated." A Christian variation is, "I was praying that God would help me get some money—and suddenly there it was." Others make their moral decisions based on who the victim was. For example, they reason that it's worse to keep the money if the person is poor than if he is rich. It's even less objectionable if it's an institution or the government that is cheated. The lament of the article was, "Nowadays Abraham Lincoln would apparently be trudging pretty much alone on his high-minded mission to return that 6 1/4 cents in change that a customer inadvertently overpaid."

What makes a child, who knows what is right and what is wrong, choose against his conscience? It has to do with the development of moral decision making.

There has been a vast amount of research done on this subject in the last few years, and most findings agree that there is a developmental pattern that influences a child to make the decisions he does.

Before two years of age the child has little, if any, understanding of right and wrong. We hope he has been conditioned or taught to respond to the word "no," but other than that he basically follows his impulses.

Between two and four years of age a child begins making decisions based on whether he will be rewarded or punished for a behavior. The child is self-centered, and his primary thrust is to do what he wants to do. His decisions are based on whether or not he will get caught and punished.

The next stage is to conform, because it is the acceptable, or the nice thing to do. Good children don't lie, cheat, steal, or disobey. Kids between five and ten many times decide what they will do because they don't want to be embarrassed or made fun of. When they choose to abide by the rules it is often because they would be ashamed if others saw them disobeying. You can see the importance of good role models and peer influence during these years. I remember when I was growing up I wouldn't think of going to a movie because none of my friends went to movies and I didn't want them to think I was a "bad" person!

During the later school years children become almost legalistic in following their own internal moral code, which to adults is not always very rational. They will fanatically defend the rules for a game, but think nothing of cheating on a test. It is during this time that they become very vulnerable to doing what authority figures tell them to do. A common plea is, "But Mrs. Jones told us we could . . . ."

This can be a very dangerous stage for determining whether something is right or wrong, because kids tend to follow a Pied Piper rather than thinking things out on their own and coming to a rational decision about what they should do. Much of the research on children who have a strong religious background and find themselves in a restrictive environment indicates that these kids tend to plateau at this level for the majority of their moral decisions, rather than moving on to a more sophisticated stage.

The final level, and the stage at which most adults should be making moral decisions, is to have an internalized set of moral principles to judge whether something is right or wrong. Individuals who make principled decisions consider questions such as: How will it affect others? What if everyone were to do this? What does God say about this behavior?

Without an internalized moral code, the child will be swept away by various pressures: the pressure to win, the pressure to be accepted; the pressure for attention; the pressure for self-gratification, etc.

How can you protect your child against the Pied Pipers of the world and help him develop a strong internal moral code based on principles?

1. Help your child feel good about himself. Kids who know they are special don't have to "buy" acceptance by saying yes to questionable activities.

2. Establish a biblically based moral code for your family. The earlier you take a strong stand as to what is right for your family, the more likely it is that your child will accept these standards and internalize them. The kids may not always like them, but they will respect the rules if they are reasonable and easily understood.

3. Encourage your child to think through why an act is right or wrong. A child doesn't start making decisions at a basic level and immediately jump to decisions based on principles. There is a pattern to the development of a child's thinking and decision making. A child making a decision because it's the acceptable thing to do is a step above the child deciding on the basis of reward or punishment. It has been found that a child moves from one stage to the next more quickly if he has many opportunities to interact with others who are making moral decisions just a little ahead of his level of thinking. Kids learn from other kids, particularly from older ones.

    Take advantage of this. Pose various moral dilemmas and ask your children what they would do and why? The rationale is a significant factor because it indicates on which level the child is making the decision. For example, you might ask, "What would you do if your family didn't have enough food and the neighbors had plenty, but wouldn't give you any?"

If the child says, "I wouldn't steal because I might get caught." He is making the right decision but for a very low-level reason—based on punishment.

If the child says, "I wouldn't steal because Christians don't steal," he is at the level of conformity, based on whether it is an acceptable thing to do.

If the child says, "I wouldn't steal because my mommy says stealing is wrong," that would be the next level—choosing not to do something based on some authority.

Finally, if the child says, "I wouldn't steal because God says, 'Thou shalt not steal,' and if everyone stole, then no one could trust anybody," this would be a principled decision.

4. Encourage your child to make his own decisions, to defend them and to take responsibility for them. Many children make decisions merely by choosing the path of least resistance. Help your child to realize that by just going along with what somebody else says, he is actually making a decision. Don't allow him to blame his buddy if things don't work out. He must take the responsibility for making his own decisions. Reinforce this fact by roleplaying a court-room scene, where the child is being accused of something because he happened to be with the kids who did it. Have him answer this accusation without blaming anyone. It's

hard to do! Our natural tendency is to blame others rather than accept the responsibility for our own decisions.

5. Don't shield your child from the consequences of a decision. When my kids were discussing what Mom should write about in this book, Kari suggested that I should tell parents to not cushion kids from the consequences of their decisions. Then she reminded me of this example. We had three free airline tickets to the Virgin Islands, so the family decided they wanted to spend spring vacation there. All except Kari. She wanted to go on a waterskiing trip with her friends. We allowed her to make this decision, even though we tried to present her with every reasonable argument why she should go with the family. One week before we left, Kari was talking on the phone to Kim, who was away at college. She realized how much she missed Kim and decided she wanted to go on the family vacation after all. I was able to get an airline ticket for her, but it was $200 more because she couldn't get a special fare. Her daddy made her pay the difference! Kari felt she learned a valuable lesson from that experience.

6. Allow your child to do things on his own. If you are constantly in control of your child's life, deciding every move he should make, the child doesn't learn much about self-control. Why should a child internalize a moral code, when the folks or the school authorities make all the decisions for him? He doesn't have to consider what is right or wrong. Many Christian kids who have attended both Christian school and public school say that they felt they had to have a stronger, more internalized moral code when attending public school because they were confronted with so many tempting situations. In Christian school, where

they weren't expecting to be confro
tions, they didn't feel the same ne'
moral code.

7. Don't always shelter your child from the windy we᷄.
Hardship develops character. Kids are a lot like my tomau᷄
plants. I had a greenhouse one year and my tomato vines
grew like weeds, but they had such spindly stems I had to
brace them. Later I noticed a smaller plant growing outside
the greenhouse, apparently from a dropped seed. I couldn't
believe the difference in the plants. The stem on the outside plant was thick and sturdy. That convinced me of the
value of a little windy weather.

When things come too easily to a child, there is no reason
to develop character traits such as perseverance, courage,
determination, or thrift. If a child never feels rejected, she
doesn't realize the value of loyalty, cooperation, and acceptance. If there has been no pain, there is no need for sympathy,
compassion and care.

Children should not be overprotected from the little stresses and strifes that may come their way. Experiencing natural or
logical consequences for their behavior, learning to cope, finding out about one's resources and abilities in life's little winds,
help to prepare a child to withstand the big storms that we all
must face sooner or later.

Research on Moral Development

I have gleaned the following general principles from the
research in character development that has been done in the
last sixty years. Don't be discouraged with these findings. Just
because the majority of kids tend to behave a certain way

oesn't mean that your child will do the same. Your child can be the Daniel who has the internal moral code to stand for right. But daring to be a Daniel doesn't happen by chance!

1. Character is specific, not general. In other words, if a child cheats in one situation, it does not necessarily mean he will cheat in all situations. Cheating strongly depends on the nature of the situation, i.e., the risk of detection, the punishment, what the child learned in similar situations, and an awareness of the implications of his behavior.

2. Knowledge and intentions do not necessarily correspond with behavior. In other words, the fact that children know what is right and plan to do what is right, does not mean they will follow through. This points out the importance of internal control. When children are warned that other kids may yield to temptation, even though they know better, they can learn to avoid strong temptations and to pray for the Holy Spirit's power to resist.

3. Children tend to conform to group standards and customs, even though these may differ from what they have earlier declared their standards to be. Note the power of peer pressure! Encourage your child to choose friends who have a positive influence on their lives rather than a negative one.

4. Children tend to be more like their friends than their classmates. The strongest influence noted in the research, came from friends who were also classmates. The closer the friendship and the more time spent together, the more influential they were.

5. Children change with age. As they grow older they appre-

ciate ideal standards and social norms, but they also become more deceptive when they deviate from these standards. So, merely knowing the standards does not guarantee better characters.

6. Resistance to temptation is somewhat related to intelligence. If a child can be encouraged to think about the moral implications of her conduct, there is a possibility that her behavior can be changed.

7. Parental and teacher influence is very important. For example, the homes which exhibit a negative parental example (parental discord, poor discipline, unsociable attitudes toward children) seem to produce children who are most dishonest. But where parental examples are favorable and the school supports the parental values, the chances of children being honest are greatly improved.

8. Actively religious families tend to produce children with well-developed characters, but church attendance or affiliation alone does not guarantee this.

9. Parental discipline has an effect on the level at which a child will tend to make moral decisions. The overly permissive parent has children who function on the lowest levels. Authoritarian practices are more likely to produce conforming or legalistic traits. Democratic discipline, however, produces kids who make reasonable decisions based on principles.

10. Friends and associates act as reinforcers and models of character, rather than originators of moral values and behavior patterns. It's your job to build the foundation.

11. Schools tend to encourage a more conformist type of behavior rather than a principled type.

    This disturbs me, especially when I look at some of the findings on why children reject religion. One of the main reasons seems to be that kids feel the authoritarian figures in their lives are too restrictive and they end up rebelling against them and God, too. If we encouraged principled decision making, rather than conformity, would we have less teenage rebellion?

12. Children need to be taught how to be good as well as how not to be bad. Parental reasoning, plus concrete suggestions for making things right once mistakes have been made, appears to be most effective in helping children develop consideration for others. Parental guidance, instruction, and involvement are all vitally important.

In summary, the research in character and moral decision making supports the importance of the IN-factors on a child's character development. The influence of close friends and the pressure to conform to group standards has been documented. Parental information is important, especially when teaching children what they should do to right a wrong they have committed. And finally, the most important of all, is internal control. It's only with a strong sense of internal control that a child can choose to be different—can dare to be a Daniel and choose right from wrong.

Chapter 7
PEER-PRESSURE PROOFING YOUR CHILD

The headlines these days are disturbing. "Teens Kick Principal." Three teens walked into a junior high school and kicked the principal in the head. Why? Because the principal busted their friend so they ganged up on him.

"Four students arrested for computer info break-in." They are accused of stealing over $3000 in merchandise by using unauthorized credit card numbers. Why? Their friend Joe needed help to steal some things.

Then there's the story about a seventeen year old who stood defiantly next to a squad car after officers frisked him and yelled, "I will never let somebody punk me or tell me what I should do." Later he added, "He can't tell me to shut up. I'll shut up when I want to." When asked about his attitude problem his mother replied, "The trouble is he's hanging around with the wrong people."

Shocking behavior. But maybe not, when you realize the almost overwhelming effect that peer pressure has on kids.

Because the influence of others has a significant impact on character, children must learn how to guard themselves from unwholesome pressures and to choose friends and role models that will help them become better people.

The Impact of INfluence

Teach about the impact of a positive influence, rather than preaching about negative ones. Help children to see how role models can significantly change their lives for the better. The story of Elijah and Elisha is a good example of this. Elisha was the son of a wealthy farmer. But during the three and a half years of famine in Israel, Elisha became familiar with the work and mission of God's mighty prophet, Elijah.

One day Elijah ceremoniously put his cloak, called "a mantle of service," upon Elisha's shoulders. Elisha immediately recognized this act as a call from God that he should continue Elijah's ministry. What should he do? He saw the nomadic life Elijah had to live as he went from place to place preaching and ministering to the people. He saw how King Ahab had hated Elijah for the things Elijah had said. He knew that if he accepted Elijah's job, he would have to live a similar life and would probably never be able to enjoy the life-style of a country gentleman. But, because of the influence Elijah had on him, he chose to cast his lot with Elijah and God's mission.

Elisha became a mighty prophet of God, but he wasn't born with this power. As Elisha lived and worked with the more experienced prophet, he became like him. Elijah's faith in God became Elisha's. When the day came for Elisha to continue Elijah's work alone, he had become so like his teacher and so filled with the same Spirit that the Bible says the sons of the prophets immediately recognized his new status and bowed before him (see II Kings 2:12-15).

The Bible is filled with stories about the importance of influence, both good and bad. Lucifer's bad influence caused Eve to eat the forbidden fruit—and then Eve's influence brought Adam's fall. The positive influence of Abraham caused his household to worship God. The negative influence of friends brought the prodigal son to his ruin.

History books, too, cite examples of how certain people have influenced others' lives. When Abraham Lincoln was a poor, backcountry boy teaching himself to read, he was given a book about George Washington. The story of this great American made an impression on him. He was struck by Washington's honesty and determined to be that kind of person. The book kindled in his heart the ambition to serve his country. Later, as his political career was taking shape, he aspired to move beyond the senate to seek the presidency—to become the kind of leader George Washington had been.

Throughout history, people like Elisha and Lincoln have become outstanding individuals by following others. And today, in every walk of life, well-known men and women testify that their success came from aspiring to be like certain individuals. The more they worked with these people, read about them, studied their behavior and speech, and learned under their expert tutelage, the more they became like them.

Ask your children whom they admire. If they could exchange places with any person in the world, who would it be? Encourage your children to take a close look at their friends, teachers, and other role models. Do they have friends like Elijah who influence them to live better lives? Do they have teachers like George Washington who can inspire them to live lives of integrity? Do they have role models that exhibit character from the inside out, or do they merely look good from the outside?

Overcoming Negative INfluences

Teach your children that they have the power to control

what influences their lives and that you will help them evaluate those influences. Don't let your children con you into thinking they aren't being influenced by their associates. They are. Maybe you can't yet detect any changes in outward behavior, but remember that character comes from the inside out. The real question is, how are friends influencing your children's thinking, motives, and desires? It's worth some serious consideration.

When Kevin was just a preschooler, he had a playmate who occasionally used foul language. One day I said to Kevin, "Kev, do you think the bad words that Randy uses are good for you to hear?"

Kevin agreed that they were bad words.

"Then, Kevin," I challenged him, "you have to help Randy to remember not to say those words, so you won't start using them."

The next day I overheard Kevin telling Randy, "You better not use those bad words when you're around me, because I might learn to say them, and then my mommy won't let me play with you because you'll be a bad example to me."

You can't be around to protect your children from every harmful influence. You must teach them to protect themselves—to have the guts to remove themselves from bad situations. Then you must support your child by helping him to fill the void with positive influences.

Evaluate carefully your children's friends and role models. It's easy to judge the kid with a Mohawk or punk clothing as "undesirable," but don't, unless you have reasonable cause. Get to know that child. Either you will find something to warn your own child about, or you will discover a kid whose looks are a statement that he is craving attention. Maybe your family can befriend this "gem in the rough"!

Teachers, principals, pastors, and church leaders can have a powerful influence on young people. You can't expect these individuals to be perfect, but don't blindly approve of them if you begin to hear that something isn't right. Keep involved. If you observe questionable behavior, investigate.

Periodically throughout childhood you might want to discuss the influence that friends, teachers, and others are having on your child. Here are some sample questions: What kind of an influence do you feel your friend is having on you? What positive things are you learning from your friend? What negative things? What kind of an influence are you on your friend? What type of friends do you need in order to become the kind of person you want to be?

Choosing Friends

Making good friends is an important task of childhood. During the preschool years, parents have a fair amount of control over their child's friends, although it can be difficult at times.

Controlling neighborhood playmates is hard. If you question their influence, insist that they play at your house where you can set the rules and monitor their behavior. Even then, things can happen that you don't expect. For example, sexual play. Children are curious about their bodies, and it's not uncommon for children to satisfy their curiosity by taking a peek at each other. But some children have been abnormally stimulated, either through viewing questionable videos and X-rated cable channels, or by seeing parents or older siblings participating in sexual acts, or by being sexually abused themselves. It is very easy for these children to engage others in sexual play that is not good. Be observant. Have an open door policy so that the doors of rooms are always left open when friends are visiting. If you discover objectionable play, don't overreact. Just calmly say, "You may not play with each other's bodies like this. Every person has private places that belong just to that person. If someone wants to see the places covered by your bathing suit, you say no. If I see you doing this again, I will not let you play together."

Friends become even more influential during the school years. That's why, as early as possible, you should encourage friendships that can have a positive impact. Here are some suggestions for evaluating your children's friends:

1. If you have questions about a certain friend, find out why your child is attracted to that person. Sometimes kids are attracted to someone because of strong, but not necessarily positive, characteristics. For example, kids that seem to have power, such as the classroom bully, are often surrounded by a close group. It's not safe to be his enemy, so some children go out of their way to be his friend. Also rich kids, or those who show off their material possessions, are often more popular. But they may have a very shallow value system prizing such things as designer clothes above being kind and polite. The rebellious child is another one to be wary of. It's very easy for the rebellion of one to rub off on close associates. For example, one mother complained her eleven-year-old daughter was being influenced by a friend in school whose mother could not control her. "I just tell my mom I don't have to listen to her. I do whatever I want and she can't stop me," was the line that her friend was feeding her. "You're crazy to do what your mom says if you don't want to!" Now, her daughter was beginning to say, "You can't make me do it!" Mom called her

bluff and then had a serious talk with her about the consequence of rebellion—and the harmful influence of some friends.

2. Watch the chemistry between your child and a selected friend. If every time they get together there is trouble, something is wrong with this relationship. Some kids egg others on to deviant or daredevilish acts. If their time together is spent arguing and fighting, then it's not productive. There is always a certain amount of bantering between friends, but it should not include hostile words and actions that are intended to hurt others. If your child ignores his chores or won't do what you ask him to do when certain friends are around, he is being badly influenced by those friends.

3. Evaluate the role models of your child's friend. It's unfair to automatically judge a child by his parents or siblings, but you must be aware of this potentially negative influence and monitor any friendship with a child who comes from a troubled home. This is especially important if you suspect drug abuse, alcoholism, unlawful or dishonest behavior, pornography, immorality, or cultic activities. Until you can assess the extent of these activities, make your child and his friend play at your house, not his.

4. Encourage your child to think about the characteristics he would like in a friend. Then help him evaluate potential friends using these characteristics. Here are some traits that could be found in a good friend.

   * Is spiritually sensitive or not rebellious against spiritual things. This is especially important for young, impres-

sionable children. As teens become stronger and have established their own beliefs, they can be encouraged to reach out to unbelievers. Many testify that it was a Christian friend who led them to Christ.

* Helps your child be a better person.

* Shows an attitude of obedience toward his parents, teachers, and other authority figures.

* Exhibits healthy traits such as kindness, politeness, courtesy, honesty, cheerfulness, etc.

* Doesn't put other people down, including your child.

* Is headed in the right direction. In other words, does he have parents who encourage him to participate in after-school sports, study music or art, or take skating lessons? Does he enjoy reading, hobbies, and have chores to do at home? Does he use his time productively instead of acting aimless?

5. Open your home to your child's friends, and make it attractive so they'll want to come often. The more they play at your place, the better you can assess whether the friendship is having a positive effect on your child. Also, if your child is having a difficult time making friends at school, having one other child over at a time helps ease the situation.

The younger the child, the more important it is that you help him find a good friend. He doesn't have to have thirty friends, but he does need one good buddy to interact with to learn the essentials of socialization! Peers should not be allowed to undo your child's good character. He should know that if you see danger ahead with one or more of his "friends," you will protect him. You will do everything possible to limit the time he spends with that friend and encourage more positive relationships. His development and spiritual life are too valuable for you to take a chance and hope that he can withstand negative peer influence. It's just not worth the risk! And the time to make this clear is early—not during the teenage years.

In addition to all the above, children should be encouraged to seek friends from other cultural or racial groups. It's in childhood that people often develop bigoted attitudes, mostly because they have never had a close friendship with someone of another culture or race.

The Role of Parental Rapport

A psychologist friend once commented that as a teen he had a couple of opportunities to have sex with aggressive girl-friends, but he resisted the temptation because he knew what it would do to his parents if they found out. They would be hurt. They trusted him to act honorably and he didn't want to violate their trust. In a study on why kids said no to drugs, the major reason given was, "I don't want to disappoint my parents."

Maintaining a positive relationship with your children during the growing years is one of the most important factors in helping them resist peer influence. Every child needs acceptance. If he has received parental approval through previous years, and this is something he has grown to value, he is less likely to turn his back on this positive reinforcement when faced with a peer-imposed temptation.

But if the relationship between parents and child has been strained, and he doubts his parents' love and their interest in his life, he will have a greater need to find acceptance else-where. Without the restraining power of parental disappoint-ment, peer pressure can be overwhelming.

If the parent/child relationship is characterized by conflict, misunderstanding, and hostility or if parents are controlling and overly strict, kids may rebel and choose to follow peers because they know it will hurt their parents. Once a child begins to make decisions out of rebellion, you can no longer trust those decisions. The better the relationship with your child, the stronger influence you will have on the decisions your child makes and the easier it will be for her to say no to peer pressure.

Drug Abuse

Kids lose control of their ability to make good decisions when they get involved with drugs. If your child is experiment-ing with drugs, it is essential that you get involved as early as possible and forcefully, if necessary, remove your child from this influence. Drugs can quickly destroy good character. And it's almost always peer pressure that initiates the drug habit.

Because the early stages of drug addiction are often con-fused with normal teenage growing pains, many parents are shocked when they learn they've been living with a drug user for a year or so and didn't even know it.

Here is the typical way that peers pull a kid into drugs. Relate this story to your early school-age kids. Warn them. Joey was twelve. Since kindergarten, he had hung around with the same three neighborhood friends. They did everything together and were basically good kids. One day when they were just hanging around, a thirteen year old from the neigh-borhood came up to the boys and pulled a marijuana joint out of his pocket. The three boys couldn't believe it. They had seen the older kids smoking marijuana. They had joked about it among themselves. But they had never tried drugs. "Where did you get that?" Joey asked.

"My big brother gave it to me," he boasted. "He and his girlfriend smoke dope all the time. Sometimes they let me smoke it with them. It feels great. You guys want to try it?"

The boys looked at each other, each wondering what the other thought, while the thirteen year old struck a match and lit the joint. He inhaled and passed it on to one of the other boys while he laughed about how great he felt. One boy tried it. Joey and one other boy said no. They were afraid of getting caught. But they watched and giggled as the other two finished off the joint. In the next few weeks, there were more and more incidents like this one. The older boy showed up with pot and one by one all the boys tried it. Even Joey eventually gave in because these were his friends. They said it was fun. And they had always done things together. At first, Joey couldn't figure out what the big deal was. He didn't feel anything—and he didn't get caught. But before many weeks, Joey was feeling it. It felt good. And still, nothing bad happened. So whenever the thirteen year old could get a joint from his brother, the boys would smoke it together. Joey was a first-stage drug user.

Most kids encounter drugs many times before they actually take the step of trying them. It usually starts in a social situation, at a party, a mall, or a video arcade, where there are lots of young people and lots of drugs. Because of their moral values, most kids are able to resist for a time, but eventually, if they keep associating with that same group, peer pressure will win out. With that first high there sets in a chemical learning sequence that makes drug users susceptible to more drugs:

"When I feel bad and take drugs, drugs make me feel good." Once they've decided that, they're in trouble, because whenever they feel low, they are tempted to get rid of that bad feeling by taking drugs.

If you find any evidence that your child has been experimenting with drugs—or is associating with kids who are—don't accept any excuses. Completely remove him or her from these questionable friends and from going to places where drugs are likely to be. If you're ever going to take a stand, do it now. Don't say, "My kid wouldn't do that," because if you do, your child will most likely get further into drugs without realizing what is happening to him.

Because drugs are so destructive to character development, you must be on guard for the first signs of drug abuse. Here are the most common:

1. Is your child beginning to dress like, look like, or talk like kids that are known to be using drugs? This conformity may show that your child wants to be accepted by this group.

2. Does your child often use eye drops because of red eyes?

3. Have things begun to disappear around the house? If you have alcoholic beverages at home, are they being used up more rapidly than usual?

4. Does your child sit in his room listening to loud rock music?

5. Does he have frequent temper tantrums where he accuses you or other authority figures of awful things?

6. Has he begun to lose interest in activities (such as sports or music) that used to be important to him?

7. Has he begun to withdraw from former friends?

8. Are his grades in school dropping?

9. Have you found pills or marijuana in his clothing or room? Don't accept lame excuses.

10. Does your teen have a persistent cough, red eyes, a sore throat, and fatigue, along with extreme emotional highs and lows? Most parents, when they begin to see some of these things, sense something is wrong. But they don't know what, and they figure it's not bad enough to do anything about. Yet, the kid on drugs is quickly losing control of his life. And the worse he feels, the more the teen craves the self-medicated high he knows he can get with drugs. The vicious cycle can rapidly pull him down. If you've observed any of these things in your child's life, don't waste time blaming it on growth pains. Confront your child. Don't be swayed by weak excuses. Your child may not tell the truth. He is not yet convinced he is hooked, so with a straight face he can swear he isn't on drugs. Ask straight kids who know him. They usually have inside information. If your suspicions are confirmed, seek professional help.

Your child cannot safely associate with anyone suspected of experimenting with drugs. The pressure is too strong. Your child may go to a counselor or a drug rehabilitation program, but if he comes back to the same neighborhood or school where his friends hang out, the chances are great that he will once again succumb to pressure from peers.

Peer-pressure proof your child by letting him or her know the influence that friends and role models can have on a life. When he is young and impressionable, help him choose

63

friends that advance his character development, and keep evaluating his choices through the years. Be sure you continue to have a positive relationship with your growing child. Finally, be aware of signs that might indicate that your child is experimenting with drugs. If this happens, your influence will be greatly diminished and he will probably have lost control of his ability to choose friends that will have a positive influence on his life.

Chapter 8
HELPING YOUR CHILD TO KNOW GOD

As important as the IN-factors are in character development, the child's relationship with God will ultimately determine his inside-out character. It's the IN-factors that can help a child choose to be a person with outstanding character, but it's Christ in the heart that makes the difference. What can parents do to help their children build a friendship with God?

Build an Accurate Picture of God

Isn't it interesting how our primary image of a person's character is influenced by our picture of him or her? I remember as a child the "mean" old ladies that lived down the block. My friends and I were sure they hated little kids, and we avoided them like the plague. As I grew by inches my concept of their meanness grew by feet. Then one day my fear was overcome by my desire to sell my quota of Campfire Girl candy, so I knocked on their door. How surprised I was when they each bought a can of candy even though they explained that they didn't like candy but wanted to help the neighborhood children! I don't know how I ever picked up a wrong impression of those ladies, but it almost caused me to miss the benefits of their friendship.

It's sad, but too often that same thing happens with our

perception of God. The childhood picture that is painted for us is often so faulty that we avoid getting to know Him. When you were young, what did you think God was like? Like your dad? Your mom? Or a favorite uncle? How did you picture Him in your mind? Was He old or young? Rich or poor? Big or little? Black or white? Bearded or shaven? Hairy or bald?

How much of your perception of God was influenced by an artist's portrayal? Was your picture of God characterized by the serene face of Jesus in Leonardo da Vinci's Last Supper, or by Michelangelo's severe God of the Sistine Chapel? How do you want your children to picture God?

God is awesome to behold. Just read about some of God's encounters with men in the Old Testament, and it's frightening to think of actually meeting Him. But that's because of sin. It's our problem, not God's!

If it were in my power to paint a picture of God in my children's minds, I would want to stay away from the Sistine Chapel God, whose stern, judgmental face sends chills even through my adult heart. I want my children to see God as the Good Shepherd looking for and loving His lost sheep. I want them to see Him as Jesus, as He said to the children, "Come to me." I want them to see a loving, understanding, considerate, forgiving, patient heavenly Daddy. But wait a minute. Where do children get their first impressions of God? You're right—from their parents! From your life—and from mine. That's a little frightening, isn't it?

In a study of more than 10,000 children in 5th through 9th grades it was found that the kid's perception of God (religion) correlated with certain behaviors. (Merton P. Strommen and A. Irene Strommen. *Five Cries of Parents* [San Francisco: Harper and Row, 1985], pp. 137-38.) If children saw God as a liberating God who accepts them just as they are and gives them the gift of salvation, this correlated positively with high self-esteem, moral internalization, acceptance of traditional standards, achievement motivation, a positive attitude toward the church and prosocial behavior. These are attitudes and behaviors that parents want their children to have. But if children saw God, or religion, as restrictive, as stressing limits, controls, guidelines, and discipline, this view correlated with low self-esteem, sexism and racial prejudice, drug and alcohol abuse and antisocial behavior.

How can you paint a correct picture of God's character for your children?

1. Live a Christlike life. When you err, point out that God isn't like you; God is always loving and kind.

2. Let your child know that God is your best friend. Let him hear you talk to Him and talk about Him.

3. Carefully select the Bible stories you tell your children, especially when they are young. It is difficult to understand God's actions in some of the Bible stories that are recorded. Until your child is old enough to realize that men choose the consequences that came to them, he could get a distorted picture of God as a God who did nothing but kill people with the flood, or destroy Sodom with fire, open the earth that swallowed Korah and his family, or turn Lot's wife into salt!

4. Never threaten your child by saying God won't love him if he's bad or that an angel is always watching him and is writing down all the bad things he does. It's important that a child feel God loves him unconditionally, when he's bad

as well as when he's good. If not, when the child makes mistakes, instead of turning to God, he will often turn away, feeling that he is so bad God couldn't possibly love him. Too many adults are struggling with this erroneous concept of God that they picked up in early childhood from naive parents who were trying to frighten their children into being good.

5. Avoid unreasonable restrictions and rigid patterns of behavior that disregard a child's needs and wholesome interests. One example is not allowing little girls to wear slacks, or forbidding a child to date until eighteen. If you find your child fearing you or trying to avoid you, perhaps you should talk with someone who can help you understand what is causing him to feel this way. If your child has such feelings toward you, the chances are great that they will be transferred to God.

6. Introduce your child to people who live the love of God. Godly persons do have an effect on children, and it may be that the children's strongest and clearest picture of God, above and beyond their parents' example and artists' portraits, will come from godly associates of all ages. Take advantage of missionaries and other mature Christian speakers who come to your church by offering a meal or housing so your kids can get to know these people. But never allow your children to think that people are perfect. Too many people leave a church and turn away from God because they have been led to believe that the people in the church should be flawless. When they find out there are a few hypocrites around, they use that fact as an excuse for turning their backs on God.

7. Help your child feel that Jesus is his best friend—an older brother. God the Father may seem distant to a child, but even toddlers can feel close to a Jesus who was born in a manger and grew up as a child. Jesus Himself said that if we know Him we will know the Father (Matthew 11:27). So, introduce your child to Jesus from his earliest years. Let Jesus come naturally into your daily conversation. For example, as you are bathing your baby you can say, "Jesus made five fingers on your hand." David C. Cook publishes a delightful series of books called "TUBable HUGables," which are designed to float in the water and include titles, *God Made Wonderful Me* and *Who Likes the Water God Made?* These books will help make bathtime fun and bring God into your child's everyday world. You can float the book and then read the story and have your child point to the fingers and toes, knees and nose, of the child in the story—just like his or her very own. Your child will learn to see God's hand in the world—and in everyday life.

You can sing songs like, "Jesus Loves Me." Try the "Highchair Devotionals" also from Cook. The titles *God Cares for Me* and *God Made My World* will introduce your toddler to the Bible in a very natural way. Put a picture of Jesus in your child's room, maybe one of Him with children on His lap, and point often to that picture, saying, "Jesus will always be with you." It's that first year that is the critical time for a child to establish faith in parents and his environment, and it is also the time when faith in God is most easily established. Don't let the first year slide by without introducing your child to Jesus, his very best friend.

8. Teach your child to be open to the Holy Spirit's influence.

Although it's quite easy to teach a child about God and Jesus through the Bible and by pointing out Godly traits in friends and relatives, it is much more difficult to teach a child to know God through the influence of the Holy Spirit. The Spirit is more abstract. It speaks to each of us (including our children) through providential daily experiences, through our meditation, and through prayer. Children should be led to understand that God's Spirit can speak most clearly to their minds when their lives are in harmony with their parents and with God—when they have nothing to hide. Indeed, when children feel good about themselves and about their behavior (when they are living a Spirit-filled life), they are eager to learn more about God.

Talk to God

You can't have much of a relationship with someone if you never talk to each other. Prayer is the way we talk to God, but too often it ends up being a mere bedtime, mealtime, and church time ritual. What our children really need is to learn how to talk with God all day long, not just when they are expected to say, "I'm sorry," "Please give me," or "Thank You."

I doubt that you would have many friends if you only talked to them when you had done something wrong, when you needed something, or when you wanted to say thank you. Relationships grow on chitchat, brainstorming, discussing ideas and plans, telling stories and jokes, sharing feelings, laughing and crying together.

Why not encourage your children to talk to God this same way? Help them express their true feelings and put a little life into their prayers. I'll guarantee that their relationship with God will grow. Here's how to begin:

70

Teach your child to be a creative conversationalist.

"Have you said your prayers yet?" one mom asked her seven year old as she bent over to kiss him good night.

"Well, not exactly," he replied. "I decided God must get pretty tired listening to the same old thing, so tonight I told Him the story of Goldilocks and the Three Bears."

Why not? I think my God would be pleased that we cared enough to share something with Him we thought He would really enjoy.

I wonder what God thinks when kids bow their heads and out tumble the same old memorized words, while their minds are on a baseball game or Susie's fancy dress? It's like saying mealtime grace by repeating the words, "Now I lay me down to sleep . . ." or blessing the food at bedtime. One little girl prayed, "God bless Bingo, Trixie, and . . ." without thinking she added, "Uncle Eddie has a farm E-I-E-I-O." When the child puts her mind in neutral and recites clichés, it's meaningless.

One night after my nine year old had prayed the same prayer every night for the last seven years, I asked, "Kevin, do you think God has ever heard that prayer before?"

"Yes," he admitted. "I prayed the same thing last night."

"Is that the only other time?"

"No," he smiled. "I prayed it the night before that, and the night before that, too."

"Kevin, do you tell your best friends the very same thing every day?"

"No, Mom. I tell them important things—like who won the soccer game and how to tie a square knot and why batteries go dead."

"Kevin, God is your very best friend. Don't you think He

might like to hear something new—something that's really important—like the things you tell your best friends?"

"I don't know," said Kevin, shrugging his shoulders, "I never thought about that."

"God is interested in everything that happens to you," I continued, "and He wants to answer your prayers. You might not be able to hear Him, but you can think an answer and then continue talking. Just to give you an idea of what really talking to God is like, pray again and I'll answer what I think God might answer."

Kevin began again. "Dear God, I had a great time with Tim today."

I answered, "God might say to you, 'Kevin, I'm happy you did. Tell me what you did together.'"

"Oh, we started building a tree house."

"That sounds like fun—and hard work."

"Yeah, it was hard work, but our tree house is safe. We braced the boards and jumped on them to make sure they wouldn't come loose."

"That was a good idea. What else did you do?"

Kevin continued his prayer. After about five minutes—which seemed like an eternity to me—I interjected, "Kevin, Mommy has worked hard all day, and I still have the dishes to do. Do you think we could say good night for now so I can get back to my work?"

"Sure," replied Kevin. "Talking to God is a lot more fun this way."

The next morning my husband asked Kevin to say grace. "Dear God," he began, "thank You for the good night's sleep—and for the terrific dream. I dreamed that we had a giant water slide in our backyard and a wave pool—a huge one just for me. It was just like the ocean. And I'm thankful we get to go to the zoo today. And please don't let me have to sit by a girl on the bus. And please help the mynah bird to talk to me. And . . . ."

By this time the girls were fidgeting. If they didn't get the food blessed soon they would be late for school. "Kevin, the food—bless the food," Kim whispered.

Obviously, Kevin was enjoying his new relationship with God, and the girls did get to school on time. The few extra minutes it took to tell God about his dream and the field trip were well worth it. It perked up our usual morning routine—and I'm sure it made God smile.

Teach your child to talk with God about what is on his mind and heart.

God wants to hear about the headlines in our children's lives. And He wants to add His commentary, if a child will just talk with Him and not at Him.

Ask your child how he feels right now: bubbly all over, crabby, impish, discouraged, silly, ready to tackle the world, like his best friend has deserted him? Tell God about it. He's interested.

To help children tune in to their feelings, have sharing times during the day. Ask the question, "How are you feeling right now?" and then together kneel down and tell God about those feelings. Before jumping up, pause a minute, be quiet with God and listen for His reaction—the Holy Spirit speaking, making impressions on your mind. Ask your child, "What did God say?" and expect an answer.

One night six-year-old Kari and her older sister were wrestling and giggling instead of going to sleep as their dad had asked them to do. When I could stand it no longer I marched into their room like a general and commanded, "Stop immediately, or you're going to get it!" Quiet reigned.

Then I asked in a different tone of voice, "Have you girls said your prayers?" They knelt down and Kari prayed earnestly, "Dear Jesus, please help Mommy not to be so strict!" She said what was on her mind, and I helped God answer that prayer by apologizing for my behavior and tucking them gently into bed with a goodnight kiss.

Teach Your Child to Pray for Others

When Kevin was four he noticed a woman I knew in a neck brace and prayed, "Dear Jesus, please help the lady with the neck cast to get it off." I thought the prayer was cute and mentioned it to the woman. A couple of weeks later Kevin received a letter, "Dear Kevin. Since you prayed for me I haven't had to wear my neck brace. Thank you."

"God answered my prayer!" Kevin shouted as he danced around the room.

It is special when God answers a child's prayers and he gets a new bicycle, but nothing can match the joy a child experiences when God answers his prayers for someone else. Help your child make a prayer list. Encourage him to pray systematically for others; teach him to claim Bible promises for those in need; keep a prayer diary and remind your youngster to thank God for answers.

It won't take your child long to find a new friend in God when he begins talking creatively with Him, sharing what's really current in his thoughts or feelings and telling God about his other friends and loved ones. Why not encourage your child to have a little talk with God right now?

Encourage a Personal Experience with God

Inside-out character either grows or atrophies, depending on your child's relationship with God. The closer the relationship, the more Christlike the character. What can you do to help your child develop a personal experience with God?

1. Share your own experience with your child.

    When children see parents having a dynamic relationship with God, it certainly makes it more appealing. Before World War II, Jan's father was a Protestant book salesman in Poland. As Jan was growing up, he never doubted that God was real because of the miracle stories his father told him. For example, one winter day his father was being chased out of town by an angry mob. As he was running across a snowy field, suddenly he fell into a deep hole and was covered with snow. He wasn't able to crawl out until much later, after the mob had lost his tracks and were heading back to town. He was then able to continue home without harassment. Can you imagine the impact on Jan and his brother and sisters when, day after day, these experiences were related to them? Surely this would be enough for Jan to have a good relationship with God. But it's not that simple. Vicarious experiences can never substitute for an experience in one's own life.

2. Help your child to step out in faith.

    Unless a child is willing to step out in faith, he will really never know how much God is willing to do for him. Your child must have a personal experience. Jan lived through the terrible years of World War II. His father was taken away to a German labor camp, leaving his mother and four young children to manage on their own. Jan saw God provide food, shelter, and protection and, after the war, a means of crossing the communist border into the free world so the family could be reunited.

Are these childhood experiences enough to last a lifetime? No. A meaningful relationship with God must be maintained on a daily basis. But you can't expect God to work mighty miracles every day, can you? Of course you can. I'd say that keeping happy all day long is a mighty miracle. Or not losing your temper. Or being on time to every appointment.

Each one of us has different needs. If we just open these up to the Lord, it will give Him a chance to work mighty miracles each day, and we'll find our relationship with God growing closer. Encourage your child to ask in faith, and expect a miracle.

3. Encourage your child to accept God's gift of salvation.

    As early as the child can comprehend, share with him the plan of salvation. A child doesn't have to be a twelve year old to understand that he is sinful, to ask God to forgive him, and to accept His gift of salvation. In fact, I believe the early school years, between seven and ten, are the years when a child is most open to God's salvation. When a child's heart is sensitive to God's Spirit, don't wait for the pastor or for a more convenient time—you can be the one to lead your child to take this important step in his spiritual development.

    When your child indicates that he accepts Jesus as his Savior, you can have him pray this prayer after you:

Dear Jesus,

I love You and want to be Your special child.

I am sorry for the wrong things I have done.

Forgive me for my sins.

And help me to obey You.

Thank You for dying on the cross for me.

I accept the gift of your life. Thank You for saving me.

I love You.

Amen.

Once your child begins to experience God's power working in his life, he'll become more sensitive to the Holy Spirit, and you'll find him more willing to make decisions based on God's will as found in His Word. And the fruit? A beautiful inside-out character.

CONCEPTS OF CHARACTER FOR KIDS

❦

A s Jan and I talked to our children
about character, we discovered that many of
the concepts were too abstract for them to
understand. We would have to make these
ideas practical and as personal as possible or
we would lose their interest. For example, how
do you explain the complexity of inside-out
character to a child? How do you get a child to
understand that developing his character is
hard work and worth the effort, yet at the same
time impossible without God's help?

Our answer to the dilemma of making
abstract concepts clear to kids was to make up
parable-type stories, read stories out of books
aloud, or use object lessons. You'll find the next
few chapters fun reading. Not only will you
gain a better understanding of these difficult
concepts, but you will get an idea of how you
can present them to your children.

Chapter 9
HAVING TREASURE
IN HEAVEN

Have you ever pondered what Jesus really meant in Matthew 19:21 when He said to the rich young ruler, "If you want to be perfect, go, sell what you have and give to the poor, and you will have treasure in heaven: and come, follow Me"? Or what about Matthew 6:19, 20, "Do not lay up for yourselves treasures on earth . . . but lay up for yourselves treasures in heaven"?

Chances are when you hear about treasure in heaven you have visions of a golden crown and a Beverly Hills mansion that God is preparing for you. If you've grown up churched, you might think of the familiar phrase "stars in your crown" that always seems to be mentioned in connection with doing nice things for others. As a child, I thought treasure in heaven meant chests of money and jewels, sort of like getting M&M's as a reward for good deeds.

What does all this have to do with character? Just this. I believe Jesus had a much deeper message when He talked about treasure in heaven than golden crowns and heavenly mansions. In fact, I doubt if He was talking about material treasure. I think He was talking about character—the treasure you are as a person. Giving everything to the poor would be for the rich ruler an indication of his true character. But he couldn't do it. Outside he looked good—he kept all the laws perfectly, but on the inside he was still selfish.

My husband, Jan, once told a story to our preschoolers that put new light on what Jesus really meant when He said to store up treasures in heaven. Why don't you drop in for breakfast, gather around the table, and listen to Jan's story. See if you discover a new meaning in the phrase, "Treasures in Heaven."

Once upon a time there were two men who were planning to go on a long journey to a land beyond a narrow, rickety bridge—.

Kim, Kari, and Kevin are eating their cereal and fruit as they listen to Jan tell another one of his original character-building stories.

"Mommy, I need some more applesauce."

"Kevin, be quiet!" admonishes Kim. "Daddy, go ahead."

So Jan continues . . . .

These two men had heard such strange and wonderful stories about the land beyond the bridge that at last they decided they would leave their houses and take the long journey to that special land. They didn't know how long the journey would take; so they didn't know how much to pack. But they did know one thing: they could take only one treasure across the bridge into the land.

The first man looked at all his belongings. "It would be a shame," he said, "to leave all these fine things behind for someone else. I've worked very hard all my life so I could have enough money to get these special items. I'll just have to take them along. What if I would need them on the trip?"

So he started packing. He packed all his clothing in his suitcase. He needed a trunk for his ice skates, his baseball bat, and his basketball. What about his TV set? He must take that—and his electric train, bicycle, skateboard, and cowboy hat.

"What about his bed and his blanket and his teddy bear?" asks two-year-old Kevin.

Oh, yes, he took those things along, too. In fact, he took so many things that he needed not only a suitcase and a trunk, but also a great big U-Haul truck.

He was anxious to get to the special land, so as soon as he was packed he got into the truck and drove off as fast as he could.

When a neighbor called after him, "Please take me with you!" he just shook his head.

"Sorry," he said, "I don't have any room, and besides I'm in a hurry."

As he swerved out onto the freeway, he nearly hit a little car that sat stranded beside the road, and he honked at the slow-poke truck that had pulled over into his lane. "Watch where you're going," he yelled. He didn't stop for anybody, and he got very angry if anyone got in his way.

Now the second man looked at all his belongings, and he remembered that no matter how much he took along on the trip, he would be allowed to take only one trea-

sure across the bridge to the new land.

"I don't really know how long the trip is going to be," he said. "Why should I take all my belongings with me? Someone could make good use of them when I'm gone, and I'll be able to take only one thing across the bridge!"

So he began to give away all his possessions. He gave all his toys to the children down the block, whose daddy wasn't able to buy them very many. He gave his nice, comfortable bed to the sick man who had only a lumpy, bumpy bed. He gave most of his food away to the poor people who never got enough to eat, and he gave most of his money to the church so it could send missionaries to tell other people about Jesus. The only things he took with him were clothing, food, and money for the trip.

After he gave everything away, he was anxious to leave. But a visitor dropped by unexpectedly and needed a place to sleep that night, so the man stayed an extra day and cooked dinner for him and let him sleep in his house.

At last when he got started on his journey, he noticed some people who needed his help. Even though he was anxious to get to the special country as soon as he could, he took time to be kind to others on the way. And every day, no matter where he was, he read his Bible and prayed for strength.

Finally, after many days, the two

men reached the narrow bridge. It was even narrower than they had anticipated, and it did look rickety!

The first man stepped up to the gatekeeper at the bridge and asked if he could have special permission to make a couple of trips across the bridge so he could carry several of his prized possessions into the land.

"No," was the reply. "The bridge is so narrow and so rickety that you can go across it only once and you cannot take your possessions."

"But I was told that I could take in one treasure. I've never been without my TV. Please, can't I take it with me?"

"No, the only treasure you can take in is the person you are!"

"But that's no treasure," retorted the man. "That's not fair!" he cried as he stamped his foot and scowled at the gatekeeper. He begrudgingly stepped aside to let the second man pass.

The second man stepped up to the gatekeeper. "Please give me all your money, your food, and your extra clothing," said the gatekeeper.

"I'm sorry," said the man. "I don't have any. I just gave my money to a woman who wanted to buy a pet dog for her little boy, and I gave my food and extra clothing to a blind man who was hungry and cold."

"Very well," said the gatekeeper. "You may take the person you are across the bridge."

The man eagerly stepped across the

*bridge and on the other side was a sign that
said, "Welcome to Heaven."*

*How beautiful it was. It was even
nicer than the stories he had heard about it.
It was worth giving up everything to be able
to go across the bridge. He hurried back to
the bridge and called across to the man on
the other side. "Give up everything. It's
worth it!" he shouted.*

*But the foolish man just shook his
head as he clung to his TV set.*

"Wow!" says Kim. "He was silly not to leave everything and
go across the bridge. He could get even better things in heav-
en."

"Yeah," adds Kari. "I'd never be that stupid."

Eager to point out the key concept in the story, Jan questions, "What was the only treasure that could be taken across
the bridge into heaven?"

"Yourself," replies Kim.

"What kind of treasure is that?" asks Kevin.

I guess Kevin's question is the question to be asked. What
kind of a treasure is your character? Is it a little tarnished?
Could you use a little Holy Spirit polish? Or is your character a
shining example to your children? And what about their characters? Are you raising them to be Christlike and to shine as a
light to the world?

We can't take our possessions to heaven. Those things only
enhance our looks and position here on earth. The only thing
that goes to heaven with us is our character—the person we
are.

"Oh," but you say, "God's going to make us perfect." In one
sense He does. He covers our sins with His robe of righteous-

ness. But in this life He provides a way to perfection by offering us the strength of His Holy Spirit to help us do what we know we should do. We've got to choose to accept this help. We must be willing to allow the Spirit to chip off the rough places and polish us into genuine treasures. The fruit of the Spirit—all those wonderful character traits like love, joy, peace, patience, kindness, goodness, and faithfulness (Galatians 5:22)—aren't zapped on us. They come as a result of our listening to the Spirit tell us how to be Christlike.

What does this mean to a child? How can you teach your child to accept the Holy Spirit's direction for his life? Ask your child if he ever thinks, "I shouldn't do that," but goes ahead and does it anyway, or "I know I ought to help my mom," but he doesn't feel like it. If the answer is yes, then those good thoughts about what a child should or shouldn't do are Holy Spirit thoughts. Most people call it your conscience. If you pay attention to those thoughts and do what you should, your character will become more and more like Jesus'. But if you slam the door on the Holy Spirit and drown out His voice by listening to heavy metal, watching bad movies, or keeping so busy you don't have time to do what your conscience is telling you, then you selfishly choose to do what you want to do, rather than what Christ wants you to do.

In regard to building character, parents have a double responsibility, for they must not only continue to build beautiful characters in themselves, but also instruct their children in the art of building beautiful characters. The treasure that we, as parents, can take to heaven will be increased when our children's characters are such that they choose heaven, too.

Paul the apostle understood this so well when he said to his children (the converts in Thessalonica): "For who could take your place as our hope and joy and pride when our Lord Jesus comes? Who but you, as you will stand before him at his coming? Yes, you are indeed our pride and our joy!" (I Thessalonians 2:19, 20, Phillips). Christian parents feel this same way. We want our children to develop the kind of characters that will allow them to choose Jesus, which ultimately means choosing heaven. If only we could make this choice for them, but we can't. All we can do is to help them develop spiritually sensitive natures.

Chapter 10
WORTH THE EFFORT

Once upon a time there were three men who started on a search for hidden treasure. Each was given a map with an X over the spot indicating the buried treasure. It led over rough rocks, through a thick forest and a boggy swamp, and finally over a steep mountain.. . .

So began another one of my husband's character-building parables. The object of this story was to motivate our youngsters to work hard on developing certain character traits that would help them be better kids. The story continued. . . .

The first man went over the rough rocks, through the thick forest and boggy swamp. But when he got to the steep mountain he said, "This is too much. I'm tired. I don't feel like going through all that hard work of climbing a mountain just to get a little treasure. I can do without that. Life is just too short to waste it searching for a treasure."

The second man went over the rough rocks and through the thick forest and boggy swamp and climbed the steep mountain until he came to the spot marked with an X. There he started digging. It was then that he discovered that he had to dig through solid rock. He chipped away a few pieces of rock and then sat down, wiped the sweat from his face, and asked himself, "Why am I working so hard? Why should I be sitting out here chipping away at this rocky ground when I could be home having fun with my friends?" So he packed up his gear and started back over the steep mountains toward home.

Now the third man went over the rough rocks and through the thick forest and boggy swamp and climbed the steep mountain until he came to the spot marked with an X. There he started digging—right through the solid rock. He got thirsty, hot, and tired, but he wouldn't give up. He knew the treasure was of such value that it was worth all the hard work and time it took to find it. So he dug and dug until at last his pick hit a box. He opened the box and there he discovered that the treasure was even more valuable than he had imagined. It was indeed worth all the hard work. From then on this man was known by all he met as the man who wouldn't give up—the man who dug through solid rock until he found the treasure and became the richest man who ever lived.

Your character is like that buried treasure. You've got to work to obtain it. Having a noble, upright character doesn't come naturally in a world that is programmed for the opposite. Let's make this practical by talking about a couple of areas where our kids are really going to have to work if they want to develop beautiful characters.

Bad Habits

An old man once remarked, "When I was a little boy somebody gave me a cucumber in a bottle. The neck of the bottle was small, the cucumber very large. I wondered how it got in there. Out in the garden one day, I came upon a bottle that had been slipped over a little green fellow. Then I understood. The cucumber had grown large after it had been put in the bottle."

Have you ever looked around at all those good, strong, and sensible adults you know and wondered why they hang onto their bad habits when they know better? Probably they are like the cucumber in the bottle. They just grew into them while young and now find it impossible to slip out of them. Changing a bad habit is work. Probably the hardest work in the world!

Much of a child's early behavior (or misbehavior) is impulsive. He sees a toy in the store that he really wants, so he takes it. He feels a little hungry halfway between breakfast and lunch and, spying the cake on the table, takes a piece and eats it. He gets angry at a playmate and screams, "I hate you." He feels sad because no one is paying any attention to him, so he masturbates or eats too many sweets because it makes him feel better. Little acts at first—little impulsive acts. But what if the next time he wants something he takes it, or if he feels hungry he eats junk food, or he gets angry and screams, or he feels sad and eats candy? What if no one is around to help him find a better way of coping with his desires and feelings, to help him control his impulsive behavior?

The answer is obvious. These acts will probably be repeated. And, like the cucumber growing in the bottle, the more they are repeated, the bigger they grow and the more difficult it is to slip out of them. Then, too, the child may begin to think that this behavior is appropriate and right. After all, he's done it as long as he can remember!

Mark Twain expressed how hard it is to get rid of a habit when he said, "A habit cannot be tossed out the window; it must be coaxed down the stairs a step at a time!" Obviously, the best way to stop a bad habit is never to start it. Since most habitual behavior originates in childhood, that is the prime time for establishing self-control and the wisdom to make good choices.

Impulsive behavior such as venting anger by shouting or hitting can easily grow into bad habits, so parents must become experts at redirecting this behavior into creative and constructive channels. After all, good habits grow in the same way as bad. When good acts are repeated, after a while they become easier. We feel good when we have done something worthwhile, and because these acts bring us pleasure and satisfaction, we tend to repeat them more frequently. Thus we grow into good habit patterns which result in good behaviors.

The older children become, the more they become responsible for their own actions. They may choose to repeat certain acts, even though they know it isn't good for them. Discuss with your children any bad habits they may be developing. Let them come up with ideas for dealing with them. Some habits may already be well established. Talk about what they should do to work on overcoming these habits before they become destructive lifelong behavior.

For example, let's say the bad habit is overeating (especially eating sweets between meals). Here is the process for overcoming bad habits:

1. Set a reasonable goal. Instead of stopping "cold turkey," try cutting down on the objectionable habit by allowing one extra piece of fruit.

2. Remind your child of the goal.

3. Figure out what situations lead to the habit, then avoid similar situations. In other words, if every time your child goes into the kitchen he sneaks goodies, keep him out of the kitchen.

4. Retrain your child. Every time he thinks of food, have him immediately drink a glass of water and then get involved with something interesting enough to keep his mind off food.

Changing bad habits is never easy, but the older a child gets, the more difficult it becomes!

Bad Thoughts and Bad Feelings

We don't usually think of feelings and thoughts as having much to do with habits. A habit is usually defined as a behavior pattern established by repetition. What then are the dangers in indulging in negative feelings and thoughts?

Feeling sad? Guilty? Depressed? Angry? "Don't worry," some advise, "These feelings will pass." Are your thoughts centered on yourself? Are you thinking about how to get even with so-and-so, or are you jealous? Today's pervading philosophy says, "Don't worry. Feelings and thoughts like these are natural." And yet we know what the Good Book says, "For as he thinks in his heart, so is he" (Proverbs 23:7).

Negative feelings and thoughts are a part of our human nature. Teach your child to recognize negative feelings and thoughts and to deal with them immediately. Do something to change those feelings and thoughts into positive ones or they can become bad habits.

Let's pretend your family is driving home from school and everyone is talking about what happened that day. Something is said as a joke that wounds the sensitive soul of your ten year old. After a few minutes it becomes obvious that there is one less voice entering into the conversation. Then you notice that Junior is staring out the window with a glum look on his face. After you get home everyone chips in to help with supper except Junior, who goes to his room. With supper on the table you call, "Junior, supper's ready," only to receive the unbelievable reply from the boy who never misses a chance to eat, "I'm not hungry." The whole family looks at each other in astonishment, "What's wrong with Junior?"

Well, Junior didn't choose to do something or say something about the offending joke when it happened. Instead, he allowed his negative thoughts and feelings to build.

At the time he was offended, he could have said, "Hey, you guys, I don't like your joking about me."

How do you think the family would have responded? "Oh, sorry, Junior, we didn't mean to hurt you," and the whole situation would have been over and Junior could have enjoyed his dinner. Instead, Junior let his feelings of inadequacy, anger, disappointment, and resentment carry him away. The feelings grew and even forced him to give up dinner, which made him feel even more miserable.

If a similar situation happens again and again, and Junior always withdraws, then it can become a destructive pattern. The initial feelings and thoughts of inadequacy, anger, disappointment, and resentment are understandable. Junior cannot prevent them. But if he recognizes these feelings and immediately does something to change them, they can be overcome.

If your child is indulging in negative thoughts and feelings you must get involved in retraining him. Try the following:

1. Allow your child some time and space to refocus his thoughts or defuse his feelings.

2. If the "blues" continue, don't let his negative spirit spoil the fun for the rest of the family. Act as if you are not affected .

3. Go to the child in approximately fifteen minutes and rub his back or just sit close. Don't plead or force the child to talk.

4. After a while, if he doesn't volunteer to talk, say, "I cannot

allow you to punish yourself with these sad thoughts and feelings. It helps if you tell someone about them. You can either tell me, or you might just want to tell Jesus."

5. If the child resists talking to you, get up and say, "I'll give you a few minutes alone." Then set a time for getting back to the family. "Do you think you will be ready to join the family in five minutes?" If he says no, say, "Then I will expect you to come out of your room in ten minutes."

6. Later, tell him how negative feelings are like brown stamps. He is a redemption book. If he lets negative feelings (brown stamps) stick to him, sometime in the future he will have to cash them in. When he cashes a lot at once, there is usually a big explosion of feelings. It's better to deal with these immediately and not let them stick. Next time you can try to remind him to deal with his negative feelings by saying, "Don't let the brown stamps stick!"

The fact is that any one act or feeling or thought doesn't form a child's character, but if these are indulged and repeated, negative habit patterns are established which can be detrimental to good character development. The moral of the story? It's easy to harbor bad thoughts and feelings. It isn't easy to choose to do something about them. But it's worth the effort!

Chapter 11
CHARACTER: GOD'S WAY

There are two basic plans for building character. God's plan, building on the foundation of Christ, and man's plan, building on the foundation of self.

God's plan is very simple. Christ is the foundation, the perfect example, and the only way we can obtain salvation. The apostle Paul says, "God's secret . . . is Christ himself; in him lie hidden all God's treasures of wisdom and knowledge" (Colossians 2:2, 3, NEB). This plan works when Christ is invited into the heart and Christ's character begins to be exhibited in a person's life. That's why it's the inside-out plan. It starts on the inside and is reflected on the outside.

Paul also realized that people have a plan—an upside-down plan—and he warned against accepting this plan with these words, "Be careful that nobody spoils your faith through intellectualism or high-sounding nonsense. Such stuff is at best founded on men's ideas of the nature of the world and disregards Christ! Yet it is in Him that God gives a full and complete expression of Himself in bodily form. Moreover, your own completeness is realized in Him, who is the ruler over all authorities, and the supreme head over all powers" (Colossians 2:8-10, Phillips).

Humanity's upside-down plan for character development is called humanism—the pervading philosophy that says you can do it yourself, you don't need help from anyone; visualize it and it's yours; think it and it will be; you don't need God . . . you are God.

It's easy to get caught up in the philosophy of humanism because we all like the idea of having power and control over our lives. And the humanistic philosophy says that you have ultimate power and control over yourself.

It's true, we do have the final power of choice. But without God's strength it's impossible to make the right choice and to have a spiritual character that is pure inside and out! Inside-out character is only possible when the foundation is Christ, not self.

Building Blocks

When my children were still preschoolers I wanted them to understand the difference between the inside-out character-development plan, which is God's plan, and the upside-down plan based on self. I did this by getting out Kevin's blocks. This is how I presented these two plans:

Man's upside-down plan starts with self. That's the foundation—the first block. This leads to pride (the second block)—recognizing self as supreme—as God. And pride leads to rejection of God's help (the third block) because man has the attitude, "I can do it myself. Just give me a good set of parents, a good education, and a few good breaks and I can do whatever I want to do in life. I don't need God. I can be good all by myself." Such an approach ultimately leads to failure (the blocks come tumbling down) which results in feelings of disappointment and despair which leads to thoughts of self, which is right where you were in the beginning—building on self! With man's upside-down plan, you can never get over the third block. The structure always comes tumbling down.

God's plan is different. The foundation is Christ (the first block) instead of self. This leads to healthy humility (the second block)—the realization that you can't do it yourself, but that all things are possible through Christ (Matthew 19:26). This attitude leads to acceptance of God's help (the third block)—help from Christ and the guidance of the Holy Spirit. With Christ there is the feeling of value (the fourth block)— the feeling that no matter what you do, you are OK because He values you, so you can value yourself. When you feel good about yourself, you are freed from constantly thinking of yourself and you can concentrate on thinking of others (the fifth block). When your thoughts are on others instead of yourself, you will be led to action—to do things for others (the last block) which is actually living Christ's love. Doing things for others is an excellent way to keep building our characters. Instead of our actions being governed by the motives of a selfish nature, they are governed by God's commandment to love Him and to love others as we do ourselves (Matthew 22:37-39).

With man's upside-down plan you can never get over the third block—pride gets in the way of asking for the help you need to resist the influences and philosophy of society. But with God's plan there is no limit to the height one's character can attain. We can shine despite the circumstances. We can have integrity amid corruption, and we can bubble over with the joy of the Lord when others are bogged down with the troubles of the world. Why? Because Christ offers us His robe of righteousness.

I never fully realized what this meant until our pastor spoke on the subject of Christ covering our good works (filthy rags of righteousness) with His robe of righteousness (Isaiah 64:6). He kept asking during the sermon, "Do I look all right?" I thought he was overly concerned with what he had worn that day for to me he looked fine in his stylish suit. Then, as he talked about how we often feel we are pretty good people, because we come to church, don't swear, and don't carry on with "sinners," he suddenly took off his jacket. The audience gasped. His shirt was torn and stained beyond repair. It looked like filthy rags. But the minute he put his jacket back on, he looked perfect. What an object lesson! Building character without Christ is like wearing filthy rags without His robe of righteousness covering us. Why don't you come to the breakfast table some morning dressed like my pastor, and see if your children don't have a new understanding of what being covered with Christ's righteousness really means!

Building Character Without Christ

Trying to build one's character without Christ is like working on actions and habits (what is seen on the outside) rather than changing the whole person. And trying to change only on the outside, which so much of character development theory stresses, is like—well, to make it meaningful to our children, Jan and I chose something they had experience with—it's just like the outer shell of rotten eggs. Here's what happened:

One day, about lunchtime, we were visiting an elderly man who had been living alone for some time. The children were hungry, and he suggested I fix some lunch for them.

I opened the refrigerator to see what the possibilities were. Some of the items looked as if they had been there for quite a while. We finally chose eggs for an omelet.

Each of my children took an egg and stood by the table waiting to crack it into the bowl. The eggs all looked the same on the outside.

Kevin cracked the first egg. "What kind of eggs are these?" he asked when he saw the white and the yolk all mixed together as a yellowish-milky substance—very different from the eggs he had previously seen.

"Oh, my—it's an old egg," I said as I dumped it into the sink and washed out the bowl.

Kari tried the second egg. Everything was fine. So Kim was next.

As Kim hit her egg against the side of the bowl, it exploded and spread a greenish yellow substance over the table and a putrefying smell throughout the kitchen.

The children gagged, covered their noses, and ran from the scene. Cleaning up that mess took every bit of motherly persistence I could muster, and as I cleaned I thought how much like character those three eggs were. They all looked the same on the outside, but it was what was inside that counted. One was a good egg inside and out. One egg was just half bad (only a few wrong feelings, thoughts, and words), but it would have ruined the whole omelet. And one egg was rotten to the core. Everything was kept inside until the shell was cracked, and then the putrefying stench affected every person in the room.

The Bible says our own goodness is like filthy rags, but I might add it is also like rotten eggs. When we try to develop character without Christ, even though the outside might appear very good, it is the inside that counts. It is the inside that reveals our true nature. Christ makes the difference. Only Christ can change the heart.

A Parable on Foolishness

Jesus taught by parables. Here's one that you might want

to tell your children about what happens when we try to do things our way, even though God offers us something better. Listen.

Once upon a time there was a man who wanted to build a house.

"I'll help you," said his neighbor. "I've built many houses before."

"No, I don't need your help. I want to do it myself," replied the man.

"But I have a special material called cement for the foundation of the house. No one else has it. It is strong and durable and will last a lifetime, if you will only use it. And I'll let you have it free if you'll just ask me. In fact, I'm willing to share it with anyone who asks."

"No," replied the man. "This is my house and I'm going to build it my own way."

So the man began to build. He mixed dirt and water together to make a sticky mud to hold the stones in the foundation. As he mixed, his neighbor came by again.

"I'm glad you are using stones for your foundation. You have some good material for building, but it will be of no use unless you can hold those stones together with cement. I'll be happy to give you more than enough cement if you just ask me."

"No," said the man. "I want to do it by myself!"

So he used mud to hold the stones together.

The foundation did look nice. No one could tell the difference—at first, that is. But soon the mud began to dry, and it wasn't sticky any-

more, and it began to crumble. And when the
windstorms came, it began to blow away. When
the rainstorms came it began to wash away.
Finally, when there was nothing to hold the
stones together, they began to fall away. And
then the house fell down and all the man's hard
work was for nothing.

Here are some questions to ask your children after telling them this story:

1. How do you feel about the man not taking any help from his neighbor?

2. Why do you think he wouldn't ask for the cement?

3. If you have some good material (like the stones) and some poor material (like the mud), what happens when you put them together?

4. If you want to build a good character, what should you do first? What should be the foundation? Whom do we need to ask for help?

Asking for Christ to help a child behave is an important resource that many Christian parents neglect.

Marty was having a difficult time with Toby's disobedience. At five years of age he just couldn't make himself do what he knew he should do. Toby wasn't rebellious, he wasn't trying to get back at his mother, he just simply chose to ignore what she told him to do—even when she made a list for him. Marty and Toby had a good relationship on the whole, but Toby's constant disobedience was beginning to wear Mom's patience a little thin. Finally, Marty got so angry at Toby that she spanked him for leaving his truck out on the front lawn overnight—

after he had been told three times to bring it in.

Toby sobbed brokenheartedly after his spanking, saying, "But, Mommy, I try. I want to be a good boy, but I can't." That gave Marty an idea.

"Well," Marty said, "maybe it's because you are trying to be good all by yourself. When Satan whispers bad things to you, like, 'Don't listen to your mommy,' you're not strong enough to tell him no. But Jesus is strong enough. Why don't we kneel down and ask Jesus to help you be a good boy and not listen to Satan?"

Marty and Toby prayed this prayer four times a day—at mealtimes and at bedtime, and Marty began to notice a difference in Toby's behavior. Once in a while he even came up to his mommy and said things like, "Satan told me not to pick up my toys when you told me to, but I asked Jesus to help me. And He did."

Successful character building comes only by accepting Christ's help. What a resource! God's plan is for Christ to be the foundation and the way. If a child tries to do it on his own, he will fail. Oh, yes, the outside behavior (words, actions, and habits) and the inside (thoughts, feelings, motives, intentions, and desires) may change to some degree, but on our own we come far short of Christlike perfection. Only Christ's righteousness can meet the requirements of God's law—that we love God more than ourselves and love others as God loves us.

The task of parents, then, is to teach their children to love Christ so the children will choose to accept Christ as the foundation of their characters and follow His plan for their lives— His inside-out plan for building their characters.

BUILDING CHARACTER DURING THE GROWING YEARS

❦

*C*haracter development is a work of a lifetime, but it's in the early years that the basic foundation is laid. There may be major revisions during the school and adolescent stages, but after that, remodeling becomes much more difficult—and more painful. It's like trying to bend the trunk of a young tree. It can still be done—but not nearly as easily as during the first few years. Understanding basic child development can help you be a more effective character builder during the various stages of your child's life.

Although every child is unique and has his own innate timetable for growth, on the average these individual timetables follow certain predictable patterns. For example, children sit before they stand; and they crawl on their tummies, then creep on their hands and *knees, and then walk. At least most do!*

Knowing these patterns may not allow you to prevent the path of destruction that may lie in the wake of a two year old as he toddles through the house. But your emotions and behavior toward the child may be checked or tempered with the knowledge that this is typical two-year-old behavior and not a maliciously evil tendency or stubborn willfulness that must be crushed out of the little rascal.

A number of years ago I came across some research that found teenage parents to be impatient, insensitive, irritable, and prone to use physical punishment. My immediate reaction was one of deep sorrow that so many children had to grow up in homes with parents who were still growing up. I was ready to start my own "Save the Children" or "Prevent Teenage Pregnancy" crusade! But as I read further, I discovered that the parents' behavior was the result of the faulty expectations they held for their children's development. For example, they expected their children to sit alone between six and twelve weeks of age, a behavior which doesn't happen until around six months of age.

What about standing up to walk? You might expect this skill at ten or twelve months, but they said they expected it to occur before six months of age! All the way down the list these parents' expectations for their babies were totally unrealistic.

The biggest shock to me was the age that teenagers expected their children to be toilet trained. Even though my husband and I tried most of the tricks of the trade—and my mother tried a few more—we were never successful in breaking the 2 1/2-year age barrier. Some parents I know have better success. They are the lucky ones! But it's not until around 2 1/2 that a child can perceive the urge in time to make it from where he is to where he needs to be, get his pants down, the lid up, get on the seat, wipe himself (hopefully without using three quarters of the roll of toilet paper), and get his pants back up all by himself. Some are still working on this skill at four and five, and it's not uncommon for six and seven year olds to occasionally lose bladder control during times of excitement or uncontrollable laughter.

So when do you think teenaged parents

*expected their children to be toilet trained?
Eighteen months? Twelve? Eight? NO! They
said at about five or six months of age. Can you
imagine how these parents must have felt when
six months, and twelve months, and eighteen
months passed and their "stubborn, willful, disobedient" child was still messing his pants! Is it
any wonder why these parents were intolerant,
impatient, insensitive, and irritable, and used
more physical punishment? They would probably react more appropriately to their children if
only they had a little knowledge of normal child
development.*

*And so it is with character builders. If
you realize how children develop and what to
expect at different stages, then you can better
understand what to teach, how to teach, and
how much your child should be expected to
modify his behavior as a result of your efforts.
That's why, in the next few chapters, you will
find the Kuzma version of a character builder's
course in developmental psychology.*

*This section has been designed as a
resource for you to use to understand what
character training is needed at a particular*

developmental stage. Therefore, you may not want to read all the chapters at once, but rather select those that deal with the ages of your children. Some topics, however, are difficult to segregate into one age level. I have made an arbitrary choice concerning the age level where this information would be most useful. So you might want to skim the entire section now and come back to the appropriate chapter when your child reaches that age level.

Chapter 12
FORMATIVE YEARS: PREGNANCY AND THE FIRST YEAR

It's amazing that during the first eight weeks of prenatal life all the essential parts of the human body, including ten tiny fingers and a beating heart, are present—and this takes place, in many cases, before "Mom" even knows for sure she is pregnant. That's why I believe you should begin your job as a character builder even before pregnancy, making sure that your baby has the best prenatal environment possible! Before pregnancy is the time to "clean up" your life, break those destructive habits, and develop a spiritually healthy life-style.

As Rudolf Dreikurs, a well-known child psychiatrist, says, "The behavior of the parents influences not only the present parent-child relationship but the whole future life of the child; it is the most important single factor in his development." And I believe this influence starts before birth.

Prenatal Months
From the moment of conception, the developing embryo and fetus is a product of both heredity and environment. The most critical time in the development of any organism is when it is developing most rapidly. For a baby, therefore, the first

few months are indeed significant.

Maternal disease, such as diabetes, measles, and syphilis, or an abnormality in the mother's hormonal system, can drastically affect the fetus. The placental wall, although a protective barrier, cannot prevent certain substances that enter the mother's body from being passed right on to the fetus. In most cases the baby actually receives a more concentrated dosage than Mom! The poisons from tobacco smoke, alcohol, and drugs are a few of the most common and most harmful substances to a baby's development. Some drugs, if taken at a significant time during fetal development may cause physical abnormalities or mental retardation; for example, thalidomide babies, or those born with fetal alcohol syndrome. How sad it is when newborns start life addicted to cocaine or heroin and must spend the first few weeks after birth going through withdrawal. Also damaging may be a mother's strong negative emotions, stress, and nervousness. Each of these affects the mother's body chemistry, which in turn affects the unborn infant.

Some professionals take a strong position that even the thoughts of the mother can affect a fetus by triggering certain chemical reactions which are transported through the placental wall and affect the cell development in the baby's brain. It has been observed by some physicians and parents that babies born to mothers who go through major crises and emotional trauma during their pregnancies are often more irritable and seem to have more adjustment problems than other babies. Even though empirical studies haven't been able to prove whether or not crisis and emotional trauma actually causes these infant behaviors, it does suggest that the baby is a product of his prenatal environment and we owe it to our children to give them the best start in life that we possibly can. It is not surprising, therefore, that even in utero the baby may be unknowingly affected by his environment in a way that will make it more difficult for him to adjust to life and, therefore, more difficult for him to develop wholesome character traits.

Why take a chance? Why not give your baby the very best prenatal environment possible? And what if you couldn't control your situation during pregnancy and your baby is due in a couple of days? You can't go back and relive those months. Put your trust in God. It doesn't help to worry about your yesterdays. The most influential years are ahead!

First Year

Watching your child develop during the first year of life is like watching a living miracle. Can you imagine, in only twelve months the child grows from a semipassive extension of Mother to an active, walking (or almost walking), talking (or almost talking), laughing, problem-solving ("How do I get Mommy to pick me up?"), game-playing ("peekaboo," "pat-a-cake," and "drop-the-spoon-from-the-high-chair"), affectionate human being? In fact, during the first year, more development and learning takes place than during any other single year of life. But it just doesn't happen overnight, or sporadically, or randomly. Each tiny building stone of development is based on a certain foundation, and this is how it happens!

Month One—Adjustment

This month is so unique in the child's life that it even has a special term—the neonate ("newborn") period, and it is characterized by the adjustment of the baby to life outside Mommy and the adjustment of Mommy and Daddy to baby!

113

Obviously, the baby is too young to learn anything. Right? Wrong! Even though the baby isn't learning that 1+1=2 or that an N and an O spell NO, he is learning about how friendly this new world is. When he cries, he probably will not remember if it was Mommy or Daddy who picked him up and fed him. However, if he isn't picked up for long periods of time, and isn't fed when he is hungry, and finally feels himself lifted roughly into the air, with the accompaniment of harsh sounds and painful blows, he will put two and two together as he continues to grow, and will get the idea that "the people around me must think that I'm not a very valuable person. This is a cruel world to live in, and living is not a very safe thing to do." So the beginning of the child's feelings about himself and others starts at birth via the treatment he receives during those first few months. If he feels loved and respected, he will learn to treat others in the same way.

Months Two and Three— *Crying and Erratic Sleeping*

Beyond the first month, two noticeable characteristics persist—crying and erratic sleeping. A significant number of child abuse cases could be prevented if parents just understood how much babies cry during the first year—and especially during the first three months. In fact, I believe that parents should be warned that crying may actually increase during the first three months (with colic and other upsets that babies seem prone to). But be comforted, there is light at the end of the tunnel. Usually, after three months the baby's crying decreases markedly. This is so characteristic that a public health nurse once told me that she offers parents a free night of baby-sitting if the baby's crying doesn't decrease after three months, and so far she has never had a parent cash in on the deal.

A baby's erratic sleeping is another thing that parents find disturbing, especially when after having already been up twice during the night they hear their "little alarm" go off again at 2 a.m. Isn't it strange that during the day the child drops off to sleep with the radio blasting, telephone ringing, and three kids running through the room, but at night you have to rock and pat and cuddle and feed and jiggle the crib and sing and . . . and . . . and . . . ? I'm amazed now, as I see how soundly my teens sleep just sprawled out across their beds, how as babies, night after night I had to stand by their cribs, my hand resting lightly on their backs, jiggling them to sleep, only to be called back on duty the minute I started to tiptoe out of their room. I know parents who even resorted to midnight rides to get their wee one to sleep—because she always fell asleep in the car but (it seemed) never in her crib.

After three months the baby's sleeping patterns become more regular. He may still demand a midnight snack and breakfast at 4 a.m., but at any time now parents may be pleasantly surprised to wake up in the morning and realize he slept through one of these feedings.

These may be frustrating times for the conscientious parent who tries to understand what the child needs or wants when he is crying and fussing instead of cooing and sleeping. But unchecked parental frustration leads to anger, and pent-up anger is what too often explodes, causing physical abuse.

What do babies need for character development at this age? The answer is: happy, healthy, loving, accepting, well-rested parents who have developed a support system so one person does not have to feel the pressure of round-the-clock, seven-days-a-week care all by herself or himself. An occasional respite from the infant's care can be provided by Daddy—or a neighbor, a grandmother, or church member, or any knowledgeable, caring, tender individual. This doesn't mean Mommy is shirking her responsibility; it just means that perhaps she can get a three-hour undisturbed nap, or a chance to go shopping, swimming, or do whatever will bring contentment, restored energy, and a renewed perspective toward the little treasure God has placed in her care.

Parents should not have to feel they must be totally responsible for the care of their infants. At least once a week Mommy and Daddy owe it to their little one to take a break together—even if it is just for an hour or two. Character develops best in a home where there is a strong and loving husband-wife relationship. Most parents do a better job of character building if they can take an occasional break and then come back to the job with renewed energy and enthusiasm.

Months Four and Five—
Reaching Out

By four or five months of age the baby is no longer the so-called "passive" infant—soaking in his environment. Now he is an active, responding, little human being, who laughs and giggles at silly people, and coos and babbles when people talk to him, and reaches out to happy faces and colorful fascinating objects.

It is usually during this time that bewildered parents discover that their infant no longer stays where they put him. This usually happens when the infant is placed on a bed or dressing table, and Father goes to find a missing diaper pin, only to discover a screaming Junior in a heap on the floor when he returns. Rolling over may not be the most efficient way to go someplace, but it's a beginning.

What do children need for character building at this stage?

Responsive, loving, caring individuals who thoroughly enjoy everything the baby does. People who play with him, talk to him, and meet his needs—even if it is in the middle of the night.

Can holding and cuddling a baby at this age spoil him? No. Spoiling occurs not because of too much love, but because of too little discipline.

Do children need discipline at four and five months? Yes. Gently, but firmly, his behavior needs to be molded. For example, when he is wiggling and you are trying to change him, he doesn't need a swat. He needs someone who will distract him from moving, and someone to say consistently, "Be still," and then gently hold his little legs and body so he can know that you are someone from whom he can learn appropriate behavior, rather than someone with whom to wrestle. This is the beginning of teaching the child that you are the loving authority of the family whom he needs to obey. This is another vital foundation stone for character development.

Months Six Through Eight— Moving Out

This is the age when a baby ceases to stay put. He perfects his rolling-over skill and immediately moves to sitting up, and crawling (which is the professionally correct term for dragging oneself about on one's tummy, lizard fashion). Creeping (which most people call crawling) is actually moving while up on hands and knees, and this occurs shortly after the child has perfected his crawling ability and practices hand-knee rocking for a couple weeks.

While the playpen is an acceptable environment for the nonmoving child (as long as Mommy is close enough to talk to, sing to, and pick up her child for a good part of the day), it now becomes a barrier to learning. After six months of age, the best use of the playpen is as a storage place for the things you want to keep the baby out of! It can also be used for safety reasons when a parent must be out of the child's presence for short times. For example, when you have to go out of the room and don't want to take down the ironing board, it is much better to put the mobile child in the playpen than to come back to an unconscious child who has just pulled the iron off on top of his head!

What do children need for character development at this age? They need parents who have a whole lot of common sense, plus a little of the wisdom of Solomon. Since babies need to move, provide a safe environment which includes childproof door fasteners and electrical outlet covers. Since babies need limits, lovingly teach some (such as, "If you touch Mommy's vase of flowers, she must put them up out of your reach"). Since babies learn through their senses, through movement, and through play, provide heavy doses of each. In summary, lovingly meet your baby's needs.

Months Eight Through Twelve— Recognizing the Familiar

By the time a baby is eight months of age (and often as early as five months) he begins to recognize the familiar things in his environment. "My blanket, my mommy, my daddy, my bed, my room, my toy." This wonderful achievement is the result of a vast amount of consistency in his life during the first eight months. This consistency now needs to be continued, because by recognizing the familiar, he also recognizes the unfamiliar, such as strangers, and is frightened by them. This may be somewhat disturbing to the parents who are eager to show off their affectionate and charming little angel to Grandma or Grandpa only to discover that Junior will have nothing to do with them, cries in terror at their slightest advance, and will only look at them from the protection of Daddy's arms or from behind Mommy's shoulder. One's natural impulse is to coax and plead and cajole, and .... But this only forces the child to retreat further into the familiar. The child's emotions can't be squelched, including the emotion of fear. These emotions must be recognized and accepted—it is the causes of the emotions that should be removed.

What else do children need to help them develop healthy characters during these months? Consistent, patient, trustworthy parents, who are willing to accept the child through all kinds of weather, who will not force the little vessel out of port, but will allow him to sail on his own natural time schedule and under his own steam. For example, don't force the unfamiliar upon him. Wait until the unfamiliar becomes familiar and then encourage him to reach out. The fact that a child is shy at this age doesn't mean he is destined to be shy throughout life. He may make a very friendly and outgoing four-year-old—if his environment is consistent and he is allowed to develop a sense of trust in his primary caretakers. It takes a heap of patience to live through these sometimes trying months—but for the child's character, it is worth it.

Fear is not the only negative emotion that creeps out during this time. Angry outbursts, although observed before, are now more frequent, louder and more embarrassing, especially when the child decides to express his anger in the middle of the sermon or throw a tantrum at the cashier's stand at the grocery store. Punishment is inappropriate at this time—what the child needs is firmness and understanding—and a good, loving example. In other words, don't spank the child. Hold him firmly against your chest and talk to him in a calm voice or soothingly sing. Try to find out what caused the problem and remove the cause.

During your child's first year the most important step for inside-out character development is for the child to form the innate feeling that, "I'm an OK person and I can trust Mommy and Daddy to meet my needs in a loving way—even though my behavior is so obnoxious it would appear that I deserve something else." This feeling of "I'm OK and my world can be trusted" gives the child the confidence and security he needs to begin stepping out and testing the limits—which is what the second year is all about!

Chapter 13
TODDLER YEARS: ONE TO THREE

If you thought the first year was a snap—it probably was. But now the fun really begins. You have begun the foundation for your child's character and now must continue building—by actively interacting with him in such a way that you strengthen his good points and improve his not-so-good ones. The toddler years are critical for teaching obedience and a love for Jesus.

The Foundation of Love
The love, acceptance, and care a child receives in the first year builds a sense of trust. When baby trusts his parents to meet his needs, he feels confident and secure and is ready to step out and see how omnipotent he really is! He is ready to actively explore his environment, and test his limits to see how much of the world he controls. He is ready to establish his independence, to develop his willpower, and to begin to make his own choices. This sudden burst of independence is somewhat startling to relatively new parents, and the tendency is often to come down hard on this "self-centered disobedient creature" and teach him a lesson or two about who actually runs the ship. Other parents will take the opposite extreme and laugh at him and ignore the testing behavior, thinking it

will go away. Either parental response, harsh or neglectful, has a devastating effect on the character development of the child. Instead of helping him to feel good about himself and confident and secure enough to continue making choices (because ultimately, making good choices is what character is all about) harsh or neglectful parents cause a child to feel ashamed and doubtful about his value.

There are two ways a child may react to a parent's harsh or neglectful behavior. One is with an inferiority complex where he feels he can't make very good choices so it is safer to allow other people to make choices for him. This can lead to overdependency on parents during childhood and, when the parents are no longer around, overdependency on peers, which can be disastrous to character development! The second possible reaction is a superiority complex, where a child will become bossy and try to control his world. He unconsciously reasons, "If I react first and control others, life isn't so insecure and frightening."

Firm, loving discipline is what a toddler needs for wholesome character development, not harsh overreactions from parents who want to rid a child of his selfish nature as soon as it emerges, or laissez-faire reactions from parents who think this is just a cute stage!

Living with Mobility

Sometime between nine and eighteen months of age, the baby learns a new skill that will significantly change his life and the lives of his parents forever—he learns to walk. Walking is such a milestone for the baby that most people now refer to him as a toddler. Throughout his second year he continues to perfect this skill so that by his second birthday he seldom falls when walking or running, can go up and down stairs without assistance, and can kick a ball. By his third birthday, he is no longer a toddler—he can jump, hop, gallop, and climb. Skipping is a challenge which he will continue working on for the next year or two. Walking, running, and galloping, or going up and down stairs is just like every other physical skill—it takes practice to make perfect. So the toddler needs safe, large spaces indoors and out where he can toddle to his heart's content.

Now, most parents are very pleased when their child learns to walk—it is the places his toddling takes him that makes them groan. Along with walking, the toddler has an insatiable curiosity, and his newfound means of locomotion carries him to such untouchables as the cleaning supplies under the sink or the family picture album. How do parents react when their innocent toddler follows his curiosity into trouble? Ranting and raving, screaming and scolding, and bellowing and blustering only make the toddler confused and bewildered. Such parental reactions leave him feeling like a no-good person and give him a bad model for self-control which he is struggling to learn. But it doesn't teach him why his behavior was unacceptable. A child's natural curiosity is essential for effective learning and later academic success. Harsh punishment crushes it.

Teaching the Obedience Lesson

To build his character, parents now must calmly and firmly teach the child that there are certain limits. You will not allow a baby to tear out the pictures in the photo album, but you can substitute an old catalog. You do not have to get up to feed or comfort your toddler three or four times during the night. Check on him to make sure he is all right, but then expect him to go back to sleep, even if he cries in protest. He will soon learn it's not worth it!

The first three years are the most important for setting a soundstage for further character development—and the lesson of obedience is the most crucial. These are the years to teach your child that you are the authority of the family. If you fail to teach this lesson during these years, then you must resort to stronger methods to show your child that what you say must be respected. You have a responsibility to make your requests reasonable. You must make it easy for your child to obey, so that during these years the habit of obedience will be indelibly etched on your child's character.

Wouldn't it be nice if all you had to do was tell your child once and he would never try the forbidden again? Well, it just doesn't work that way. At least not immediately. But here are a few pointers that may help you to be effective as you teach the character-building lesson of obedience:

Teach Your Child What NO Means

First of all, put up all the untouchables you possibly can so that you won't have to say "no" all day and end up missing half of his offenses. Instead, you'll be able to concentrate on catching him trying to touch those things that can't be moved. Then when the child reaches out to touch something he shouldn't, startle him with a strong, "NO!" If he looks back at you and smiles (which some one year olds have the nerve to do) and starts to touch it again, say "NO" even more strongly, pick up the child and remove him from the temptation. If the willfulness of your child surfaces again, and testing Mom becomes a game, a swat on the hand should get the "I mean what I said" message across. But avoid this if you possibly can.

Start the obedience lesson with simple requests when the

child is in a cooperative spirit.

For example, "Come to me." "Give me the soap." "Please pick up the ball." Then reward your child for complying. Smile, say "thank you," and let your child bask in your approval.

Make Sure You Can Enforce What You Ask Your Child to Do

Don't start the obedience lesson by asking your child to go to sleep, eat his dinner, stop crying, or urinate in the toilet. You can't enforce those requests and make your child obey, because you can't control his emotions or body functions. Start teaching the child the obedience lesson by making requests that you can enforce. "Shut the door." "Take off your shoes." "Put your head on the pillow." These requests can be enforced. For example, if he resists shutting the door, you can take his hand, lead him to the door and push it shut, while saying, "I told you to shut the door, and I meant it."

Make Your Request Clear

Make sure your child hears and understands. Get your child's attention before you speak.

If the child doesn't obey the first time, repeat the request as you move to enforce it. "I said wash your face with this cloth," and begin to wash the child's face. Or impose a consequence. For example, if the child throws a toy, simply take it away.

Make Your Request Positive

Don't start your request, for example, with the command, "Don't" or "If you . . . ." Kids don't hear the "Don't . . ." or "If

125

you . . ." but just tune in on the ". . . hit him again," and so they do.

Have Only a Few Rules, But Consistently Enforce Them

I suggest three basic commandments: (1) You may not hurt yourself. (2) You may not hurt others. (3) You may not hurt things. You can have more specific rules spin off from these basic three as your child develops more verbal understanding. "You can't run out in the street because you may not hurt yourself." "You may not hit Baby because you may not hurt others." "You may not throw a ball in the living room because you may not hurt things." And be consistent so your child isn't confused about what the rules really are.

Disciplining Objectionable Traits

Around the first birthday objectionable traits begin to appear. After the child's second birthday, if not before, you can be sure to notice such things as whining for an ice-cream cone, or pouting because it isn't forthcoming, or sassing when Mommy tries to explain the reason why there is no ice-cream cone. Every child I know has tried these "control" techniques at least once in his lifetime—and if yours hasn't yet, watch out! Your time will come.

How you handle these objectionable traits the first time they appear will determine whether they will be used again. Here are some helpful hints.

1. React calmly and firmly. "You may not whine in this house. It is not acceptable."

2. Give the child the positive thing to do. "Smile and say

please and you'll be surprised how much more it will bring you."

3. Take control of the situation—don't let the child control you. "You are whining because you think if you whine enough that I'll give it to you. But you are wrong." Reasoning or trying to talk the child out of whining, such as, "Why are you so sad? Don't cry, I can't stand it. What else will make you happy?" etc., is usually ineffective. The more time you spend arguing, the more the child feels he is in control.

4. Let the child know that if he doesn't change his behavior immediately, you will do something about it. You may say kindly but firmly, "Stop whining now, or I'll take you to your room."

5. Don't reward the child by giving him your attention while he is exhibiting negative behavior. Act decisively and quickly to help him change his behavior rather than try to reason with him when he is in a foul mood. If the unacceptable behavior continues behind his bedroom door, don't let the family pay any attention. Instead, do something exciting with the family. You must let the whining, pouting, or sassing child know that his behavior hasn't hurt anyone but himself.

6. Confront the child later. After tempers have cooled and you are giving him a back rub, or he is snuggling against you in the rocking chair, if you think the child is able to understand your reasoning it may be appropriate to say simply, "I know how badly you wanted the ice-cream cone. Next time talk to me about it. I'll try to work something out so you

will be happy. But if you whine, you will get nothing."

These are rules for the one and two year old, the child who is seeking to find out who he or she is, who is becoming independent and autonomous. This child must at the same time learn about what "society" (his mother and father) expects of him, and what it considers right or wrong. Obviously, a child who is well-trained at this point will be much easier to guide in the years to come. But the task is far from finished. I guarantee that the parents of preschoolers are in for a few surprises.

But before we move on to the preschool years, I have a few suggestions about the spiritual instruction you will want to provide for your toddler.

Spiritual Instruction

Introduce your child to Jesus. Your instruction can be through stories, songs, and simple object lessons in nature. For example, as you look at a fluttering butterfly, you can say, "Jesus made the butterfly for you to enjoy, because He loves you."

There should be good books for toddlers at your local Christian bookstore. If not, ask them to order some of those suggested in appendix B.

Now is the time to make church a regular part of your child's life. Take your child to the Cradle Roll division for an age-appropriate program. If your church doesn't have a program for toddlers, then maybe God needs you to get one started!

Don't expect your child to sit still through the worship service. A toddler is programmed for movement! Some parents have helped train their child for a quiet time by starting a daily "church time" at home, where Mom sits with her children and provides books or quiet "church" toys for the child to play with while she listens to a Christian radio program or a tape. This may help train your child for church, but there is no money-back guarantee if it doesn't work! If your toddler isn't "wired" for church time, don't try to force it by making unreasonable demands and then punishing the child for "disobedience." Just leave the service and go to another room or outside. Look for ways to talk about God while your child plays. A flower, an ant, or a pebble can all remind us of God's love. You want your child to love going to God's house, not fear and resent it.

If your church provides a daily age-appropriate lesson study plan for your child, follow these lessons at home. Learn the children's songs that are sung at church and reinforce them by singing them with your child throughout the day.

Let your child see you pray and, as his speech increases, have him repeat a prayer after you. He'll soon be praying on his own, even if it's just "Dear Jesus. Amen!"

Chapter 14
PRESCHOOL YEARS:
THREE TO SIX

The preschooler is generally an active, spontaneous, inquiring, imitating, playful person eager to please parents and adults. During these years he gains a basic understanding of how his world functions, he develops important motor skills, and he begins to step outside the shelter of the family to make new friends.

The preschooler is verbal enough to give you a run for your money and make you wish for earplugs for Father's Day. In fact, by the time a kid is five he has mastered most of the basic rules of language, and his speech, except for a few mispronunciations and persistent grammatical errors, resembles that of an adult.

If you listen carefully, you'll hear some real gems. For example, a little girl was playing house with a four-year-old boy. After they had put all their "children" to bed and laid down to go to sleep, she turned to "Daddy" and whispered, "Shushhhhhh, not now, the children might be listening."

If you are a parent of a preschooler, you probably have a notebook full of priceless comments like this one!

By the time a child leaves the preschool years, his conscience is active—although not necessarily acted upon. His basic values have been established, and the foundation for his character is pretty well intact. These critical years between three and six are like finishing school for a child's character. The window of opportunity is still wide open, but around seven it begins to close.

So take advantage of the fun and frantic years of trying to convince your child that Mr. Rogers really can't look out of the TV set and see him in his pajamas, that the rainbow's end is not in the middle of the next field as it appears, or that milk really does come from cows and not from stores. Enjoy these rich and wonderful years.

Reacting with Love

When your child was a tiny baby, you may have found it quite easy to respond to his shortcomings with perfect composure. But as he grows and you feel he ought to know better, it becomes progressively more difficult to keep cool. That's why so many preschoolers are yelled at or spanked when, in most cases, he is old enough to be reasoned with or learn from consequences.

Reacting to your child with uncontrolled anger or harsh criticism can retard a child's character development, for it teaches a child that he is only loved when he does exactly what Mom and Dad say. In the majority of cases, of course, parents love their children all the time, but that is often not the message children perceive.

"If I'm good," he reasons, "my parents will love me. If I'm bad they won't."

One marvelous picture book has the little one asking something like this, "Mommy, how can you love me when I'm so bad?" When Mommy responds, "I love you all the time," the little one tries to discover the reason.

"Because I obey you?
"Because I'm so smart and talented?
"Because I do kind things?"

Finally Mommy says the magic words that every child is hungering to hear, "I love you all the time, because you are mine!"

What a priceless message! (See Miriam Schlein, *The Way Mothers Are* (Chicago: Albert Whitman, 1963).

When a child feels loved only when he is good, he may develop hostile feelings, especially toward authority figures. Also, because the child's picture of God is in the formative stages, he may begin to think that God loves him in the same way. "Good" behavior which is motivated by fear rather than love can result in a child's making moral decisions merely on the basis of whether he will be punished, which is a very shallow reason for choosing between right and wrong (see chapter 5). For optimum character development, children need to feel loved just because they exist, not because of what they do.

If love is what God's character is all about, and if you want your children to be loving, then you must learn to treat them in such a manner that they will have no reason to doubt your love.

To determine whether you are showing unconditional love to your children, compare your actions to the criteria of love in I Corinthians 13: 4-8. Here is what God says love is:

Love is patient, kind, does not envy, does not boast, is not proud, not rude, not self-seeking, not easily angered, keeps no record of wrongs, does not delight in evil, rejoices with the truth, always protects, always trusts, always hopes, always perseveres, and never fails.

It almost makes you feel guilty, doesn't it, when the list

starts out with being "patient," has is "not easily angered" in the middle, and ends with love "never fails."

Impossible!

But now is no time for guilt. Put those feelings away and move forward with a renewed commitment to love.

If the sixteen characteristics of love in I Corinthians 13 are too many for you to remember, I have an idea. Reduce them to their lowest common denominator. I did, and discovered five traits:

CARE

RESPECT

ACCEPTANCE

FORGIVENESS

AND TRUST

Each starts with a letter from the word CRAFT. So all you have to remember is that C is for Care; R is for Respect; A is for Acceptance; F is for Forgiveness; and T is for Trust. (See Kay Kuzma, *Filling Your Love Cup* [Parent Scene, P.O. Box 2222, Redlands, CA 92373].)

To evaluate just how loving you really are, ask yourself the following questions and consider how you would respond in these different situations:

C = Care

Do my words and actions give my child the message that I don't really care, even though I say I do?

Sally came home crying, "I don't have any friends."

Daddy's response was, "It's no wonder, the way you treat them."

Was this a loving thing to say? No. It showed a lack of care and concern for Sally and made no attempt to look behind

Sally's statement to find out what the problem was and how it could be solved.

The caring way to handle this situation would be to say, "I'm sorry you are so sad. It hurts when you don't think you have any friends, doesn't it?" Then give Sally a hug and sit down to talk about how to solve the problem.

R = Respect

Do I always treat my child with respect?

Johnny hit his sister. Mom came in, grabbed him by the arm and shook him. Was that a loving thing to do?

No. You won't grab someone by the arm and shake him in anger if you respect him. Instead, stop Johnny and firmly say, "You may not hit your sister because you may not hurt others." Then listen to Johnny as he shares his feelings.

A = Acceptance

Does my child feel she is accepted even when she misbehaves?

Four-year-old Mary was angry and screamed, "I hate you." Mom just ignored her. Later, when Mary apologized, Mom continued to ignore her.

Was that a loving thing to do? No. What type of rejection is worse than a parent not even speaking to you—especially after you have apologized?

To show your child acceptance, you don't have to approve of every action. But when you disapprove, mention the specific behavior you can't allow. Say, "I can't let you scream, but if you tell me in a soft voice why you are angry, I'll listen." Don't criticize the child by saying something general like, "You're just a sassy kid."

F = Forgiveness

Do I really forgive my child for mistakes and forget them, or do I keep bringing up his past errors?

Tony didn't feel like helping his dad, so he ran and hid in the tree house and didn't answer when Dad called. Tony got punished and said he was sorry. Now, whenever there is work to do, Dad says, "Where is that boy? He is always avoiding work. Tony's just lazy."

Was that a loving thing to say? No. Bringing up past mistakes and making it sound as if Tony can never change is certainly not showing forgiveness. Give a child another chance and expect the best.

If the child feels his mistakes will never be forgotten, he will take pains to blame others instead of accepting responsibility for his behavior and saying "sorry." The long-term result is a burden of guilt.

T = Trust

Do I trust my child to make appropriate decisions?

When Billy was two he took a piece of candy from a store. Now, every time Billy goes shopping with Daddy, even though he is almost four, he is made to empty his pockets as soon as he is outside the store. Is that a loving thing to do?

No. It doesn't show trust. Of course there is such a thing as reasonable suspicion—and we shouldn't stick our heads in the sand when it comes to moral issues—but suspicion shouldn't last for two years following the only episode of wrongdoing!

A Child's Self-Centered Nature

Young children are even more concerned with themselves than adults.

Their thinking is egocentric, or self-centered.

Another word to describe this same attribute is selfishness, and most of us consider selfishness a sin.

Since the fall of Adam and Eve, all children have been born with this self-centered, sinful nature. But they aren't born sinning! It's not a child's fault that he is born with this nature, so punishing him for something he can't help doesn't accomplish anything.

It only causes stubbornness and rebellion.

Our job in building character is to understand the nature of a child and help this child move from self-centered thinking— where he believes he is the center of his world—to more mature or principled thinking where God and others become his primary focus.

This is what character development is all about: it's a life-long struggle against our basic, selfish natures.

Once you understand a child's self-centered way of thinking, you will realize why preschoolers get into so much trouble. For example, some children get into squabbles with their friends quite easily. With two self-centered children reasoning that they are right, it is no wonder that "friendly" disagreements may escalate into blows. As their ability to talk things over increases, they rely less on physical aggression to get their point across.

So, encourage your child to express his feelings in words by saying, "You may not hurt someone else, but you can tell him how you feel."

Another example is that almost every preschooler will try a little lying and stealing on occasion. Parents should not view this behavior as the beginning of a lifetime of criminal activity, nor should they punish severely for something the child did not know was wrong. The young preschooler's reasoning is such that if he holds something, then it is his; or if he says something, it is true.

This again is part of his self-centered thinking and must be treated with loving firmness rather than anger. "I can't allow you to take something that belongs to someone else. Tell me first when you want something. We'll talk it over and decide if it's something we want to buy."

When your child does take something that doesn't belong to him, you should make him return it or pay for it. This is the way the child begins to learn about ownership and property rights. But don't shame your child!

Don't allow your child to believe that everything he wishes or thinks is true. Correct him, but don't make a federal case out of his "lie." Simply comment, "Saying something does not make it true. I know you spilled the milk. Here is a cloth to wipe it up."

Fantasy playmates are often part of an imaginative preschooler's life. Don't panic and don't try to logically convince your child the playmate isn't real and he's lying. Simply say, "It's fun to pretend." These playmates serve a purpose. When the child is lonely, he has someone to talk to; if angry he can vent his feelings on his "friend" without hurting others; when tempted, the imaginary character can be the "bad boy" without your child getting into trouble or he can be a child's good conscience. If you don't give undue attention to this fantasy it will pass when the need for it no longer exists.

The big problem during these preschool years is to determine when stealing and lying have become more than just a stage that preschoolers go through. If after age four or five these behaviors continue fairly regularly for six months or more, then something other than the child's self-centered nature may be the cause.

You need to discover the reason for this behavior and treat it. It might be that the child knows this disturbs you, so when he's angry this is what he does to punish you. He may do it to get attention. It may be that the child feels he has to have things to be accepted, or that the world owes him the things he takes.

You may be so harsh in your punishments that he feels it is safer to lie than to own up to his mistakes. Stealing and lying can become habitual if not dealt with properly at this early stage.

Teaching a Child to Share

Because of a young child's self-centered thinking, it's difficult for him to share.

He naturally wants everything for himself, and when he has it, he thinks it is his. Don't expect immediate success, but by eight years of age you should be seeing a more generous spirit—in fact, if you're not careful he may be giving away things you really don't want to be given away. (Generosity peaks at about eight years of age.)

But until then you are going to need some suggestions to cope with his selfishness. Try these:

Let the child own his toys.

You can't share if you don't have anything that is yours. It's only when the child experiences the pride of ownership that he can begin to understand other people's property rights—that it is wrong to take something that

139

belongs to someone else.

Don't force your child to share.

The more you try to force a child to share something, the stronger is the tendency to resist. If the object belongs to the child, let him control it. If it belongs to you or someone else, then the owner should decide what is to be done with it.

Make it easy and fun to share.

When a friend comes and wants to play with your child's toy and your child won't share, don't say, "You're selfish." If your child feels that you think he is selfish, he will continue that behavior.

Instead, say to the other child, "That toy belongs to Jamie. He will share when he is finished, but until then let me show you this other toy." Then make the other toy interesting enough to be accepted by the other child.

When Jamie loses interest in what he is playing with, you can say, "Jamie, if you are finished playing with your toy, why don't you tell your friend she can play with it now?"

Then reward Jamie for sharing by showing how pleased you are. Theoretically, this is supposed to work. But if your child has real trouble in this area, you might want to have a few things that you own just for visitors to play with. Then you can control who plays with them.

If two children are fighting over who gets to play with a toy, put it out of reach.

Say, "If you children can't decide how to share the toy and play peacefully, I'm going to put it up and no one will get to play with it." This gives the children extra motivation to work on solving the problem rather than merely getting their own way.

Show your child that you enjoy sharing.

Be willing to share things with your children. Let them see your generous spirit with others. It may take a couple of years, but your good influence will have its effect.

Understanding the Preschooler's Reasoning

A young child judges whether something is wrong by the harshness of the punishment received or by the extent of the consequences, rather than by motives and intentions.

For example, a preschooler usually thinks that breaking a stack of plates, even though by accident, is much worse than breaking a small plastic cup out of anger, because more plates were broken than cups. Judging motives and intentions, those gray areas, usually comes only after six, seven, or even eight years of age when the child's reasoning ability has developed sufficiently. You must be careful not to reinforce his immature thinking by imposing harsher punishment on a child for breaking a stack of plates, even though he was trying to help you, and ignoring the cup broken out of anger.

If you are interested in testing out your child's thinking in this area, tell him the following story about two boys, each of whom found a wallet filled with money:

"One boy gave the wallet to his daddy so his daddy could

find the owner, and his daddy spanked him. The other boy took the money out of the wallet and bought himself an ice-cream cone. Which boy was the naughtiest boy?"

More than likely a young child will say it was the boy who got the spanking.

Why is this, when it is clear that stealing is wrong?

Young children judge an act by the consequences. If the consequence is good, like getting an ice-cream cone, they conclude that what the child did must be good. If the consequence is bad, like getting a spanking, they conclude that what the child did must be bad.

Because a child's immature reasoning causes him to come to conclusions based on consequences alone, you must be very careful not to become angry at your child's innocent mistakes or you will reinforce his belief that motives aren't as important as behavior.

Be considerate. Search for his motives. If his motives were innocent—or even honorable—hold your punishment. Instead, teach him more responsible behavior without resorting to anger and harsh discipline. It may not change his thinking immediately, but you will be laying the proper foundation for him to accept the idea that character is more than just outward behavior.

How Preschoolers Learn

Preschoolers learn by doing, by getting dirty, by being involved. Allow for messy play and hands-on experiences.

To develop character, make object lessons out of real things, roleplay, or let children participate in character-building activities like making a gift for someone or accompanying you as you volunteer your time to put together food baskets.

Preschoolers are sponges. Let them see you demonstrate the character traits you want them to develop.

They're insightful, too; they can discern hypocrisy! Be careful that you don't say one thing and do another, or do good deeds merely to be a good example even though you would rather be watching TV!

This is the age when children can begin learning from other people's experiences. What better way to teach them about appropriate ways of behaving than to tell them stories from the Bible or read to them stories of other children's experiences. Frequent your Christian bookstore or church library and bring home books which are appropriate for the age and which teach Christian values.

Preschoolers learn through games. Play the "What if . . ." game with them: "What if Johnny told a lie about his friend, Steve, because Steve wouldn't let him play with his wagon?" "What if George stole a package of gum?"

Or play the "Finish the Story" game: "Andy and Todd were climbing a tree and Andy tore his new church pants . . ." Let your child finish the story.

Play the "How would you feel if . . ." game: "How would you feel if I yelled at you in front of your friends?" "How do you think I would feel if you got angry at me and said you were going to run away?" Playing games is an effective way to bring up potentially hot issues and discuss them without putting anyone on the spot.

For more ideas about how you can actively teach important character traits, see the sample plan for developing character traits (appendix A).

Another characteristic of the preschool child is that he is constantly thinking of new things to do, new things to make, and new activities to try. He is bubbling over with ideas.

Children need a variety of materials to play with, and a variety of creative experiences to try. They need dress-up clothes, dolls, large trucks, and tricycles so they can imitate adult roles—sort of try them on and see how it feels! Through this type of play they begin to understand how others feel.

Sometimes their dramatic play gives a real insight into how life is perceived by a youngster. For example, a four year old scolded her doll harshly for spilling her milk and then began spanking her for not cleaning her room. Mom almost interrupted to say, "That's no way to treat your doll," when she recognized the inflection in her daughter's voice—it was just like hers!

This sudden burst of dramatic and original play should bring understanding and encouragement from Mom and Dad.

If Junior is always told he is too messy, too noisy, too silly, and is constantly criticized for his shortcomings and failures, it is likely to lead him to develop feelings of self-deprecation and guilt. Your job as a preschool character builder is to provide a loving atmosphere where your child catches the message that he or she is loved unconditionally.

Encourage her to apologize when she is wrong, and let her know that she is forgiven for her mistakes. Accomplishing this will allow her budding conscience to be free to grow, rather than being burdened down with a premature load of guilt.

In addition, now is the time to begin a more formal plan for character building, choosing those traits that you want your child to develop and designing ways to teach them (see section IV).

Make character training a part of your daily schedule. The earlier you begin to "bend the twig," the easier will be your job!

Chapter 15
EARLY SCHOOL YEARS: SIX TO NINE

What a joy it is, after working so hard and praying so often and planning so carefully to guide a child's character development, to at last wave good-bye to your six year old as you watch him walk down the path toward school.

Time for a break?

No, indeed no. Even though I believe that the first six or seven years of a child's life have more to do with forming character than anything in the future, your job as a character builder is far from finished. If you quit now, chances are that a great deal of what you have accomplished will come unraveled in the wear and tear of school life.

Although the home continues to be the most important educational center for the developing child, school (which includes the influence of both teachers and peers) has a major impact on children. That's why many parents are choosing to teach their children at home rather than risk the possibility of an unhealthy environment outside the home.

If a child has had faulty character training at home, then a poor school environment can do him in. But even a good school environment will not be able to compensate for negative family influences.

The winning combination is to have a positive school experience built upon a good home foundation. When this happens there can be continued growth toward God's ideal—inside-out character.

Protect Your Child from Feeling Inferior

The most meaningful gift you can give your child as he steps outside your door and heads off to school is the assurance that he is a very important and capable person. This protects him from the vibes of inferiority he may soon get from social failures:

"Mommy, Cindy won't play with me."

Or academic failure:

"Daddy, I'm afraid I'll forget how to spell D-O-G when the teacher asks me."

Of course, the younger the child is when he enters this foreign environment, the fewer skills and abilities he will have to make friends and to succeed in various learning situations. Don't force your child into a situation he or she is not mature enough to handle.

Boys, especially, are less mature than girls at five and six. Just because your child doesn't start school with the rest of the neighborhood kids doesn't mean he isn't as smart! Don't feel forced into conforming to what society has suggested is the age children should start school. Seek the guidance that is available from your school system.

Do what is best for your child. There are many factors that go together in determining school success. Then do everything you can to make the first few years of school successful. You have invested too much in your child's character to have it sacrificed in a school situation that makes him feel inferior.

When children feel inferior, they may tend to withdraw, be aggressive, act silly, or exhibit any number of "coping" behaviors. They will also tend to conform to peer pressure rather than stand up for what they have been taught is right. What school-age children need is enough self-worth to go against the crowd when it comes to a moral issue, and that is very difficult for school-age children to do because their acceptance by peers is so important to them.

Your best insurance for a healthy start in school is to establish a positive relationship with your child's teacher. Show your interest and willingness to cooperate. Keep involved.

After School Activities and Supervision

Because school-age children are finally more of an asset than a nuisance when it comes to helping around the house, parents may tend to impose a heavy dose of household chores.

As they get older, school homework gradually increases. This is also when children are branching out into extracurricular activities such as tumbling, tennis, swimming, piano playing, or horseback riding.

Then comes Scouts or church clubs. Make sure your child doesn't try to do so much working, studying, practicing, and socializing that she has no time for family life or for quiet moments to herself. All of the extra activities are good—but too many may be detrimental to the developing child.

Parents must be careful to encourage—but not to push.

Kids need time to think, to doodle, to read fun books or listen to music. Basically, kids need balance. And it's these years when parents still have some control that balance can be built into a child's life.

School-age children need Mom and Dad. It is a fallacy to think that children should take care of themselves just because they can take care of themselves during the time between the final school bell and the sound of the parents' car coming up the driveway after work.

Some children mature earlier than others and enjoy some time at home alone. But others, even into their teen years, are lonely and frightened when alone.

Basically, school-age children need supervision and direction. If you can't be there, make sure someone is around to give your child the guidance he needs. Idleness can lead to misbehavior and experimentation with forbidden activities, such as smoking, drinking, or stealing.

Don't take a chance.

Getting Kids to Do 'Home' Work

Doing useful labor around the house is an essential part of a child's character development. It teaches kids to be responsible, it helps them develop worthwhile skills, and it reinforces the truism that nothing worthwhile comes free.

Having a house, a car, pets, or a yard takes work. Having a fresh strawberry pie for supper takes work—either you work for wages so it can be purchased, or you make it yourself. One of the biggest conflicts between school-age kids and their parents is over doing chores. Some parents feel that the hassle it takes to squeeze a little help out of a child isn't worth it. But it is.

You just have to learn techniques of making work at home attractive, meaningful, and fun.

It may help you to follow these suggestions:

1. *Trade a privilege for a responsibility.*

   Keith resented his dad's calling him home to do various tasks when he was in the middle of a game with his neighborhood buddies. He wanted the privilege of staying until the game was over.

   Okay. Trade a privilege for a responsibility.

   "Keith, you may play with your friends each day until suppertime without interruptions as long as your room is clean, your practicing done, and the dogs fed before you go out to play."

   Guess what?

   Keith happily fulfilled his responsibilities.

2. *Never call a task a chore.*

   The word "chore" sounds dreadful enough to scare away any normal kid. Plus, it communicates the idea that home responsibilities are a drudgery and something to be avoided.

   Rather, call it a job, a privilege, a joy, an honor. Anything but a chore.

3. *Make the job a challenge.*

   Every four year old I know loves to do the dishes—but very few ten year olds do. I'm convinced that the difference is not the age so much as the challenge of the task. At four, doing the dishes is a fantastic challenge. At ten, it's a bore. The challenge at age ten is cooking the dinner that dirties the dishes.

   One day I needed Kevin to clean out the ashes from the fireplace and sprinkle them under the trees in the grove.

He balked.

So I tied Missy (our dog) to the wagon and had her pull the wagon load of ashes for Kevin. Before I knew it Kevin was back, complaining that there weren't more ashes! It was the challenge that made the difference.

List the jobs your child is required to do. Then, consider how you could make each task challenging.

With some, like taking out the trash, it's difficult. Maybe you could occasionally trade one of your challenging jobs for a less challenging task on your child's list.

Kids have to learn that some tasks have to be done whether they are challenging or not. It then becomes their responsibility to make these routine tasks challenging by seeing if they can do them faster or better than ever before.

4. *Start the training early.*

If your child has never been required to do anything around the house during the first six years, don't be surprised if he rebels at being assigned home responsibilities at age seven. Encourage him and let him know that you really do need and appreciate his help.

5. *Work along with your child.*

If you are even semi-fun to be with, chances are your child would rather work with you than work alone. The more happy and positive you are, the more your kids will enjoy your companionship. What better way to share your values than when you work on a task together? But avoid criticizing and nagging.

Make this time the most pleasant time of the day.

6. *Give your child a choice.*

   Don't give him a choice whether or not to help around the house, but a choice of which task to do. "Would you rather vacuum the carpets or wash the car?"

7. *Offer an incentive for quick, efficient work.*

   Often the reason children hate having a job to do at home is that they dillydally all day long so that the job is never done and is forever hanging over their heads.

   How much better to encourage them to get right in and get it over by saying, for example, "You can go swimming as soon as it's done."

8. *Encourage rather than criticize.*

   When a task isn't done right, or when something goes wrong, such as breaking a dish or spilling something, don't make matters worse by telling the child how stupid it was to do that.

   Rather, help him get out of the mess and ask him how the mistake can be prevented from happening again. Ask him what he learned from having to do the job over. He will, you hope, have learned that if something is worth doing, it's worth doing well.

9. *Occasionally reward children for work done well.*

   Every task done well deserves a word of appreciation. But should you give anything more?

   Don't feel that an occasional reward will make a child think he should always be paid. Rewards come in all

sizes and shapes. A hug might be just as effective as a
dollar bill. But if the child is saving his money for a new
bicycle, what a nice surprise extra money would make—
especially if you would have had to pay someone else to
do the job if he hadn't done it.

10. *Expect only the level of performance appropriate for his age.*

In other words, you may have to accept less than perfection as a "job well done." Remember, you have many
years of practice behind you, while your child is just
beginning. It is the attitude with which the task is done
that is the most important, not necessarily the skill.

Making Healthy Decisions

Many school-age behavior problems would disappear if
children learned to live a moderate, healthy life. Life-style does
affect behavior. Too much sugar, too much stress, not enough
sleep—these things are important.

I wonder why so many kids have difficulties in this area?
The example of their parents' life-style wouldn't be the problem, would it?

Many children do not know how to handle the independence they have when they go to school and are away from
their parents' watchful eyes. They are increasingly influenced
by other children's behavior and, in addition, they now have
spending money of their own. Too many reason, "Mom will
never know if I throw away the apple she put in my lunch and
spend a quarter on ice cream at the store."

I believe in prevention.

Tell your child, "You are going to be met with a variety of
new temptations as you go to school. These will compromise

what you know to be healthy. For example, many children do not make wise decisions and spend their money on food that is not good for their bodies. You are going to be tempted to do the same, but remember what you have been taught, and we know you will make wise decisions."

Bad eating habits can start during the school years if the cupboards are filled with junk foods and parents are not home to monitor a child's after-school eating.

Obesity is a major problem now among children. Also, many kids don't get enough exercise. One of my physician friends was involved in a fitness screening at a local school, and he was shocked at the large number of children who were in such poor physical condition that he was afraid to let them get on the treadmill!

Don't allow your child to get into the habit of coming home from school, grabbing a snack, and sitting down to watch TV for the rest of the afternoon. To maintain healthy bodies they need to be riding their bikes, playing soccer, or mowing lawns!

These are the days when "slumberless" parties are in fashion, or a kid wants to stay up past his bedtime to finish reading an interesting book or watch a TV program. Don't be so rigid in your bedtime demands that your child is forced to be deceptive and read his book using a flashlight under his covers or sneak down to the study to watch TV without your knowing.

Not every child requires the same amount of sleep; some are night owls while others are early birds. But you must make sure your child gets enough rest during these growing years so that he is not irritable and contrary.

Once a reasonable routine has been established kids can begin making their own decisions, within certain limits, about when to go to bed.

If you have discussed and together have set policies that pertain to your child's health, such as the amount of sleep that he needs, you'll find your child making better decisions.

Why? He understands the underlying reason.

But if you allow your child to make choices about health issues entirely on his own, don't be surprised if she is swayed by peer pressure, regardless of the health principles that you have established in your home. Not until these health policies become part of a child's internal value system will they be strictly maintained.

And what do healthy decisions have to do with character development?

Just like the apostle Paul said in I Corinthians 6:19, our bodies are temples for the Holy Spirit. To make sure your child clearly perceives the Holy Spirit's counsel, it is important that his mind isn't clouded by unhealthy practices. And it's usually during the early school years, when a child has less parental supervision, that unhealthful habits are formed.

Going to the extra effort it takes to get your child off to school on the right track will certainly make character building a great deal easier as she grows older and more independent, and as you find your influence on her life diminishing.

But it's not over yet!

You've still got a lot of hard work ahead as your child moves through the next critical stage on his or her journey toward adolescence.

Chapter 16
LATER SCHOOL YEARS: NINE TO TWELVE

By the time your child is in the fourth or fifth grade, he probably will be encountering some school-related problems that may affect his character. Two of the biggest problems many children face are that of homework and the temptation to cheat.

What about Homework?

Homework can be a real character builder! It almost forces the child to develop IN-Factor #3—INternal control. But if your child is having trouble with internal control, you might appreciate some suggestions from the real experts in this field—my kids. Here is what they say is guaranteed to work.

1. *Take away the TV.*

   TV and homework don't mix. But if you say no TV until the homework is done while the rest of the family is watching TV, the child with the homework can easily feel resentful. In fact, many lie and say their homework is finished or hurry to write down any answer just so they can watch TV with the rest of the family. Don't put this type of pressure on your child. If your child is having problems in this area, make it a family policy to not watch TV on weeknights. You'll find that the less TV your family watches, the less they will crave it and the more time they will have for reading and other profitable activities. If there are special programs that you don't want to miss, record them. When the homework is done early, celebrate. Pop some corn, cuddle up in a fluffy quilt, and watch the recorded show.

In some families kids are more addicted to video games than to TV, and they may need some parent-imposed limits that are similar to those established for the TV.

2. *Be tough on your kids during the early years.*

I was really surprised when Kevin made this suggestion, because I was remembering all those nights that we "sat on him" to make sure his homework was completed. Now it's paying off. He has finally caught on to the fact that he can get good grades, and people think he's smart if he simply does all his homework—and does it on time. Once kids get the taste of success and realize how important homework is, don't keep bugging them by asking, "Have you done your homework yet?" Let them assume this responsibility.

3. *Get teacher cooperation.*

In larger schools kids can get lost in the crowd. Sometimes the first a parent knows about a child's delinquent homework is at a parent/teacher conference weeks after school started! Don't be a delinquent parent. If you sense your child should be doing homework, but he never brings any home, check with the teacher and get a progress report. Don't let your child think he can fool you. Some children have real difficulty remembering assignments, especially if they are given verbally. It may not be willful loss of memory. It may have to do with the way their brain functions. If this sounds like your child, have his teachers write down all the homework assignments and send them home. You can sign the note and return it the next day. When parents and teachers cooperate, the child isn't tempted to say, "I didn't know I was supposed to do that."

Also, if you find that on a regular basis your child doesn't know how to do his homework, then something is wrong. Talk to his teacher immediately.

4. *Give your child a break and an energy boost.*

Don't make your child start his homework immediately after school. Let him take a break as long as it's not TV. Let him ride his bike, play outdoors, or work on models. Some kids need an after-school energy boost, especially when lunch is eaten at 11:30 A.M. Set limits though. I suggest only fresh fruit or a fruit drink. No soft drinks or cookies, which give a quick boost and a quick letdown just when the child is ready to start homework. My kids love fresh fruit slushes. (Frozen strawberries and either lemon or a banana whizzed up with lots of ice. Eat immediately.)

5. *Link homework to a privilege.*

   In other words, if the child really wants to do something, say, "Not until your homework is done." My kids said they didn't like this idea, but it works. I certainly see more concentrated effort when Kevin knows he can have his cousin come over, "as soon as your homework is done."

6. *Reward good grades with something special.*

   My kids have liked this idea, but it doesn't work very well with younger children who need immediate gratification. Many children reason that it's not worth the extra effort to get good grades if they have to wait five months to get a reward. Our best success was when Kevin came up with the reward he wanted for certain levels of achievement: A tennis racket for a B average; a surfboard for a 4.0. (He is still working on that one!)

7. *Help your child plan good study habits.*

   Let him choose a quiet place where he wants to study. Some kids are desk kids and some aren't. There is nothing wrong with the floor—if that's where Junior wants to be. In most cases the radio, even with mellow music, is distracting. However, some children actually concentrate better with the radio blaring. Don't ask me how they do it, but I can't argue with success. If your child wants the radio on, trade this privilege for a responsibility. "You can have it on if your homework is completed by eight this evening. If not, you lose that privilege tomorrow."

Make sure your child has everything he needs so he doesn't have to waste his study time running around getting a drink or trying to find a sharp pencil. And help him by not planning parties, shopping trips, and other interesting things at times he needs to be doing his homework.

8. *Help your child, if necessary.*

I know there is a school of thought that says parents should never help their kids with homework. It's the child's responsibility, not yours. But I also know that kids hit some pretty big obstacles that can be discouraging if they don't have parental support.

9. *Let him do his homework with a friend.*

Believe it or not, some kids are more motivated when they have a friend around. Friends can encourage and occasionally help each other. But studying together can also be a disaster! Carefully monitor this one.

10. *Make sure your child feels good about school.*

If the teachers are all down on him, the principal calls him a turkey, the coach says he's a wimp, and the kids tease him, why should a child be interested in homework? It's extremely hard to pump motivation into a discouraged child. Every kid needs someone at school who believes in him, who thinks he's great, and who sees the potential under his mischievous behavior. If your child is in a no-win situation and his self-worth is wilting, drastic changes need to be considered. Get your child to a counselor. Find someone to tutor him who treats him with respect. Change schools. I can't tell you exactly what you should do, but your child's character is at stake. Negative feelings about school authorities, if not solved, can generalize to others, including civil authorities. Do something so that this doesn't happen.

I'm not saying that the way to solve a school problem is to escape. Sometimes the most effective character building comes when a child must cope with and overcome a bad situation at school. But he may need some ideas. For example, when Jason was in junior high he had a teacher that required "perfect" obedience and demeaned anyone in class who had a creative idea or whose behavior was not letter perfect according to her certain standards. When Jason and a few other boys didn't come up to her standards, she made life in class pretty miserable. But they weren't about to change because they could see her unreasonableness and her inconsistency—allowing some kids to get away with things while lowering the boom on others.

Then one day Jason's family read a story from *Guideposts* about a teacher who felt so insecure that she was extremely strict because she didn't want to lose control. Jason asked, "Do you think that's Mrs. Jones's problem?"

"It could be," agreed Mom. "If it is, then every time you boys challenge her it probably makes her feel more insecure, and she clamps down even harder. Maybe you should try to help her feel secure. Compliment her on her good points instead of persecuting her about her bad ones and see if it doesn't make a difference."

That is exactly what Jason started to do. He saw his teacher in a new light. She was feeling insecure, just as he did sometimes. When Jason started treating her with respect, Mrs. Jones changed. She never became Jason's favorite teacher, but the major problem was solved. That's character building!

Cheating in School

Cheating is a major problem in school—and there are no easy answers. Chances are that even your child will cheat or be tempted to cheat when other children are doing so, especially if there are no consequences and if he has a strong internal need to achieve. You must prepare your child to resist the temptation to cheat by talking to him about difficult situations in which he may find himself. Sometimes it helps to roleplay what he should do in a given situation, so he won't be tempted to violate his personal moral code.

Years ago I came across a study I'll never forget. The researchers wanted to determine how a child's inner need to achieve would affect the decision to cheat. They set up a target with various points assigned, depending on how close the child came to the bull's-eye. The researchers gave each child a "laser" type of gun, but one which wouldn't indicate to the child where he or she actually hit the target. Instead, the kids were told that the "sensitive" board would register their hit and flash on the screen the points they received. They were to record their scores for ten tries and give the secretary their total score. She would give them their prize.

If a child got 75 to 100 points he got a gold star badge that said "Expert," for 50 to 75 points a silver badge that said "Good," and for less than that the prize was a sticker that said "Fair." Obviously, every child wanted the expert badge.

Then the researchers left the room, leaving the child alone to record his scores. The numbers that flashed up on the board were extremely low numbers. Almost every child cheated to try and raise his score, but those children with the greatest internal need to achieve cheated the most. In other words, if 2 flashed up on the board they would assign themselves a 9 or 10, while a child with a lower need to achieve would only put a 5 or 6.

And what's the moral of the story? We can push our children towards cheating if we, as parents, have unrealistic expectations of how well they should do. Interesting, isn't it?

Of course some children seem to have a built-in need for perfection and a competitive spirit that keeps them on top. But what could be positive may end up being detrimental to character development if they think they have to cheat in order to reach their own standards.

Talk to your school-age child about these pressures, and encourage him or her to take a personal stand to be honest and trustworthy. Stress the fact that integrity is far more important than grades.

Keeping Open Channels of Communication

As your child nears the teenage years, be prepared for some rough times ahead. I consider the best preparation to be a parent-child relationship that is built on mutual love—care, respect, acceptance, forgiveness, and trust—and where as many conflicts as possible are peacefully resolved or avoided.

The best way to avoid conflict is to keep tuned to your child's ups and downs and to handle the little things as they come up, rather than thinking everything is fine only to discover that you are sitting on a powder keg which is likely to explode no matter which way you move.

Every school-age child needs time alone with one, or preferably both, of his parents each day even if only for five or ten minutes. Encourage your child to share by asking specific, but open-ended questions. "How did you feel when . . . ? What was the most interesting thing that happened in school today? If you had one thing you could do differently today, what would it be?" Don't ask, "What did you do in school today?" The question is too general. Every kid I know seems to do nothing all day in school.

Don't try to pry information out of your child. He is beginning to establish a private world of his own that he doesn't want to share with his parents. This is a normal and healthy step towards independence. Respect it.

Family communication can be improved by starting family councils where the child is included in the decision making—especially those decisions that affect her. Kids are much more compliant when they know you have carefully considered their opinions.

Let your growing child know that you are on his side. When he comes home grouchy, sympathize with him about the hard day he must have had, rather than telling him that he is acting like a baby. When his behavior gets on your nerves, don't blow up, just give one of those famous "I-messages": "I feel angry when I find your wet towel lying on the floor." An "I-message" points out the behavior you don't like, but the emphasis is on how you feel about it. Contrast this to the "You-message" which condemns the child: "You are always leaving your wet towel on floor. When will you ever learn?" This technique is absolutely essential if you want to continue to build character during your child's teen years.

What is the answer for character development during these years? Maintaining good rapport is essential. Be friendly, helpful, and actively involved in your child's life even though he spends a great deal of it away from home. Think ahead and prepare your child for what could become character-compromising situations. Continue to encourage his good traits and modify those that are detrimental to good character. And continue to model the kind of behavior you want your child to cultivate.

Ahead . . . well, hang on. The teenage years may be the most challenging of all!

Chapter 17
TEEN YEARS

I found an interesting quotation the other day. The author stated, "Our youth now love luxury. They have bad manners, contempt for authority, and disrespect for older people. Children nowadays are tyrants. They no longer rise when their elders enter the room. They contradict their parents, chatter before company, gobble their food, and tyrannize their teachers." Sounds like they need some character training, doesn't it? But hold on, this wasn't written about teens today; it was written about kids some 2,300 years ago! And the speaker? Socrates!

It's shocking how little youth have changed through the generations.

But I still think teens are a great group of kids, in spite of their occasionally immature behavior. I love their energy, their drive, and their willingness to question values as they search for meaning in their lives. I find them open, frank, and honest, yet sensitive to others—especially their peers. And they have a great sense of loyalty. I see them thinking seriously, working industriously, and playing enthusiastically. They are a courageous bunch of kids, willing to stick out their necks for what they believe is right; willing to crusade for a better world.

But I also see kids who have lost their way and have grown alienated from their families. Kids who are experimenting with mind-altering drugs, lawless behavior, and sexual perversion. My heart cries for them—as well as their moms and dads back home praying for them.

What can we do to protect our youth so their characters don't crumble under the pressure of an upside-down world?

The answer is to understand something about their development so we can effectively meet their needs and keep the lines of communication open between the generations. During these critical years, parents who want to build character must be allies, not enemies.

Understanding Sexual Development

The time between the beginning of a child's adolescent growth spurt (ages eleven to fifteen—earlier for girls than boys) and physical and sexual maturity (eighteen to twenty-one) is often a rocky period for both parent and child.

Mom was putting some freshly laundered clothing into Tony's dresser drawers when she came upon a crumpled piece of paper—a page torn from a sex magazine. The sight of nude bodies engaged in pornographic sexual encounters was enough to age Mom fifty years! She glanced over at Tony sprawled across his bed, absorbed in his math homework. Her "innocent" little boy with these pictures? What should she do?

She knew that Tony was beginning his adolescent growth spurt, which meant the rapid development of certain sexual characteristics (pubic hair, beard, lower voice, wet dreams, etc.) and an increased interest in the other sex. Because these changes affect every aspect of the adolescent's life, they can be bewildering, especially if he is not prepared for what is happening to him.

Mom knew that her son's feelings about his body and the changes that were occurring would be tempered by the sexual knowledge she and her husband had given him from early childhood and would continue to offer during this period. She wanted him to feel that all parts of his body were good and that God created his body so that certain parts were pleasurable to touch.

She knew that if kids understood that it was normal to be aroused when an attractive person of the opposite sex was close—or even viewed in a picture—he would not feel guilty about these strange new feelings and could learn how to make positive decisions about how to control his actions. She knew all this, and yet she never expected to find sexy pictures in her son's drawer.

She decided it was a good time for a talk. "Oh, Tony, I notice you have a picture here in your drawer of a man and a woman doing things to each other," she said as if she were talking about why robins sing and bees make honey. "You probably had some questions about the picture when you saw it."

No comment from the suddenly serious math student.

"If you want me to explain some things about the picture, I'll be happy to," she said as she put it back into the drawer.

"You will?" questioned Tony, not really knowing whether to believe his mother!

"Yes," she said. "When you see a picture like this it probably makes you feel strange inside. You're naturally curious to find out what is happening." She then went on to explain that people make a lot of money selling these kinds of pictures, but looking at them can cause you to want to do the same things that you see, and that's not good.

She continued, "God gave the sexual experience, which we call sexual intercourse, to a man and a woman to be a symbol of a lifelong commitment to marriage. He made sex to have a special feeling of excitement and pleasure, so a husband and wife would want to have sex over and over again to remind them of their commitment to each other. Marriage means two separate people coming together as one. And sexual intercourse is when two people are the very closest physically. When a man and a woman get married, they are like one flesh—like one person—until one of them dies.

"But Satan doesn't like happy marriages, so he has taken this symbol of commitment and made a counterfeit so that it wouldn't remind people of God's ideal. Sex in our society often doesn't mean very much, and many don't even realize that it is a symbol for a lifelong commitment to marriage. They just think it is something to do because it feels good.

"Pictures, like the one in your drawer, help Satan because they cause people to want to experience the exciting pleasure of sex immediately, even though they are not married or their marriage partner is not around. There are two ways that Satan counterfeits God's beautiful symbol of a lifelong commitment to the person you are married to. First, by getting people to have sex with lots of other people. Pretty soon the act has little, if any, meaning. That's why you may sometimes hear guys bragging about how many girls they have had sex with. When these people get married and have sex with their spouses, sex won't have the same meaning of a lifelong commitment. They are depriving themselves and their mates of something very special. But once it's given away to the wrong person, you can never get it back. Does that make sense?"

Tony nodded, still in shock that his mom was being so open, but he was listening.

"The second way Satan counterfeits this beautiful symbol is by influencing young people to experience this exciting sexual feeling by themselves. And that's called masturbation.

"You see, Tony, God designed sex to bring two people together in the closest relationship possible. Masturbation does the exact opposite. Instead of drawing you close to another person, you isolate yourself. You don't want anyone to know you are having sex with yourself. Kids learn how to stimulate themselves. Then whenever they feel a little down or lonesome, they masturbate. It can easily become a habit. It's not wrong to touch yourself, but if you continue to have sex with yourself, it won't have the same meaning as it should when you are married. In fact, many people end up finding that they can have a more exciting time by themselves, so they choose to masturbate rather than have sex with a spouse. When this happens, instead of sex bringing two married people closer together, it separates them."

Tony asked a few questions at that point, and Mom tried her best to answer. Then without Mom saying anything, Tony got up from his bed, went over to the drawer, pulled out the picture, tore it up, and threw it away in the wastebasket saying, "I'm not going to look at that junk again."

It's sad, but I doubt if he was able to keep his word. Unbiblical sexuality (sex outside of marriage) is an open way of life in today's society. Just by flipping on the TV you are likely to hear about or see somebody going to bed with somebody other than a spouse. But at least Tony now had a sensible reason to say no the next time he was confronted with sexually explicit pictures.

That's healthy sex education. And that's what our kids need if they are going to continue to build strong moral characters. It is very important that teens have a clear understanding about sexual anatomy and physiology to understand the reproductive system and how pregnancy occurs. Information about AIDS and other sexually transmitted diseases should be given, even to good Christian kids. In addition, children should be allowed to read good books telling about kids who have chosen to have premarital sex and have faced the consequence of becoming parents before they were ready. Very few teenagers see beyond the cuteness of a baby to the almost overwhelming responsibility of providing 24-hour-a-day care to a helpless infant.

Teens need to discuss why kids say yes to sex when they would really rather say no. Reasons like: "I didn't want to disappoint him." "I felt guilty because I flirted with him and led him on." "I was afraid he wouldn't like me if I said no." "I was bored; there was nothing else to do." "She wanted to do it, and I didn't really care." "I just wanted to have the experience." "I was dared to do it, and I didn't want to be called a chicken." "We were high on pot, and it just seemed the thing to do at the time." Encourage teens to think of a reply in case they are ever confronted with lines such as "Everybody is doing it," or "If you really loved me you would go to bed with me."

Youth should also understand that each individual develops at a different rate and that this has nothing to do with one's masculinity or femininity. Girls who develop early, before their parents have thought to give them adequate information, are particularly vulnerable to the advances of older boys; and late-maturing boys suffer, worrying whether or not they are normal.

In addition, teens should understand enough about the other sex to know how they respond sexually. Girls should know their behavior and clothing, or lack of it, can turn on a guy so he's ready to have sex immediately. Is this really fair?

Boys should understand that girls who seem eager probably don't want sex; they only want to feel close to someone. Also, a girl may feel obligated to say yes because the guy has spent so much money on her. How else can she repay him?

They should also be aware that sex never happens without a buildup. When dating, it's safer to stay with a group of kids. Make a policy never to go with someone to an empty home. Girls should know that most rape is committed by a friend or an acquaintance. Watch the hugging, kissing, and touching. Encourage kids to set limits before they get themselves into what might be a compromising situation.

Parents not only have a responsibility to provide correct information about sex, but they should also provide a wholesome example of the enjoyment that can come from married life. If one's own marriage relationship has been less than ideal, or if there has been a divorce, teenagers can still be encouraged to observe the positive aspects in the lives of family friends. Marriage should be seen as such a beautiful experience that complete sexual gratification is worth saving for it.

Independence

If parents have built character well, then by the time the child is fifteen (going on eighteen), they should be able to sit back and enjoy the person they have been molding. Now is not the time to begin major revisions or additions. This will only force the teen to prove her independence by her rebellious acts.

Remember the five aspects of love: *Care, Respect, Acceptance, Forgiveness, and Trust?* This is the time for parents to make it clear that they love their child by trusting him to make his own choices whenever appropriate. This doesn't mean that teens need no parental counsel, encouragement, and advice. They do, but it must be given in a way that shows the growing child his parents trust him.

There is, however, one area that kids may need more protection than they think. That's the area of morality. Teens should be told that Mom and Dad will step in and make a decision if they see their teen about to do something that they don't have adequate knowledge and experience to deal with. In other words, you won't allow your kid to sit in a parked car until 3 A.M. or have a party in your home without adult supervision.

Believe it or not, kids respect parents who will stand up and be counted at critical times, especially if they refrain from complaining about every little error of judgment the teenager has made. Teens like being able to have their own way—but they respect parents who maintain reasonable standards.

Independence from parental control should come gradually. When it comes too quickly the teen is not prepared to handle the responsibility. It is best if the teen knows that his parents have a plan for setting him free so that he will not have to rebel to gain his liberty. Every year should bring him a step nearer to independence from his parents. For example, perhaps in the thirteenth year the teenager will be completely responsible for the care of his own room. When he's fourteen, he can choose his own wardrobe, within certain budget limitations, and by the time he is fifteen he can decide how to use his time, as long as he abides by reasonable family policies and continues to carry his share of home responsibilities. The gradual lengthening of the apron strings should continue until the teenager reaches eighteen and is making virtually all of his own decisions.

Such a plan, however, is doomed for failure unless your teen is taught early how to seek out the information needed to make good decisions, how to weigh the alternatives, and how to accept responsibility for choices. It takes practice to become a good decision maker.

Maintaining Good Relationships

A major challenge of the teenage years is to find one's identity. No longer are teens satisfied to be known as so-and-so's daughter or a chip off the old block. And they may go out of their way to prove it. They seem to become supercritical of adults and other authority figures, and are often impatient with others' imperfections—while failing to notice their own.

During the early teen years, parents are still legally and morally responsible for them. The fact that rebellion is a recognized part of adolescence does not mean that parents should do nothing to stop rebellious behavior. Very few teenagers really like themselves when they are rebelling, and they will respect parents who take the necessary time and energy to explain the responsibility God has given to them to guide their children and to curb their harmful practices. There are certain consequences to rebellion (this was even true in heaven), and parents have a God-given responsibility to make this clear to their children. One father, a very busy physician, left his office in the middle of the day with a line of patients waiting to see him to travel twenty miles to his home to talk to, pray with, and properly discipline his teenaged son for showing disrespect to his mother. After the incident the boy had a changed attitude and even thanked his dad.

To make life go more smoothly for families with teenagers

and to round off the sharp edges of the adolescent's developing character, parents and teens should master the following three skills:

Skill #1. Give I-messages followed by contracting for change.

I-messages communicate feelings without taking on the tone of blame that one gets with a you-message. One time as I was riding in a station wagon with friends, I overheard a conflict between a father and his fourteen-year-old son that could have been avoided if they both had used this skill. In preparation for traveling, Father pushed the button to raise the rear window which Junior wanted left open. Indignantly the son shouted, "Dad, what do you think you're doing? Stop it, will you?" (you-message).

His father was somewhat taken aback and replied, "I was raising the window so the gas fumes wouldn't come in" (I-message). This seemed to be a reasonable answer given more calmly than the majority of parents probably would have done. So I was shocked when the son continued his sarcastic comments.

"You must be crazy. Nobody believes that one anymore. You are always making up stupid excuses like that!"

Everyone in the car was stunned. Not even the father knew what to do, so the subject was dropped. But one more I-message from the father would have been instructive. He could have said, "Son, I feel hurt and embarrassed when I hear words like that." By using the I-message technique, the father could have corrected his son, even in front of guests, without his son becoming defensive and embarrassed.

If the son had learned the technique of using I-messages,

he could have expressed his feelings without being disrespectful to his father. For example: "Dad, I had my hand on the window and I would have liked to have it left open so I could feel the breeze."

This conversation could have been immediately followed with a suggestion or a contract something like this, "What if we leave the window down until the car is aired out, and then put it up when we get on the freeway?" If the teenager didn't like that suggestion, he could have been encouraged to make a countersuggestion until father and son arrived at a compromise solution without being critical and disrespectful to each other. This illustrates what Thomas Gordon calls a "no-lose" method of working with older children. Parents and teenagers need to read Gordon's book *Parent Effectiveness Training* together, and then both begin practicing the suggested techniques.

Skill #2. Learn to persuade instead of push.

No one likes to be pushed, forced, or manipulated. When parents begin controlling their kids, kids rebel. In fact, parents don't want to be pushed either. That's why both generations need to learn the art of persuasion.

Notice the difference between persuasion and push in these two examples where Dad wants his daughter to take a summer job she doesn't want to take.

Dad #1: "Why don't you want to take it?"

Daughter #1: "I want to be home this summer with my friends."

Dad #1: "That's silly. You can still see them, just not as often. You're being foolish to let this job opportunity pass. Other kids would jump at the chance. I can't believe you are so stubborn. If you don't take the job and earn some money for college, I'll just have to charge you room and board."

The above is obviously the pushy dad. Now let's see how another father might handle this situation.

Dad #2: "I can tell you feel uncertain about the summer job."

Daughter #2: "Yes, I want to be home this summer with my friends."

Dad #2: "I can understand that. Have you considered what other jobs are available? You might want to compare the pros and cons of various job possibilities. What would be some good reasons for taking the job? How do your friends feel about only seeing you twice a week? Here is the name of someone who held this job last summer. You might want to talk to her about the demands of the job. I know you can make a good decision when you consider all the options carefully."

Notice how Dad #1 told his daughter what she should do and used demeaning language filled with you-messages. He was trying to threaten her into accepting the job. Dad #2 tried persuasion. He asked questions to stimulate her to think about the possible options, and he offered information that would encourage her to make a good decision. Which dad do you think is ultimately going to be effective?

The persuasion process also needs to be mastered by teens. Kids who tell their parents what is going to happen ("I'm going to go to a party Saturday night whether you like it or not.") are sometimes shocked when they find themselves grounded. But parents can be persuaded—if kids learn the technique. "Mom, there is this neat party Saturday night at the Browns' that all my friends are going to. I know you wanted me to spend Saturday night with the family, but this party is really important to me because I've been wanting to get better acquainted with some of the kids in my class. Is there any way we could change our family plans so I could go to the party? I have Mrs. Brown's phone number in case you'd like to give her a call about the party. Thanks, Mom, for understanding." Do you see the difference? I'd give in and let her go, wouldn't you? Parents can be easily led—if teens would only master the technique!

Skill #3. Learn to be ADULT in your interactions.

A wonderful motto for teens and parents is to never needlessly harm the respect of another.

For this philosophy to become a part of everyday life, you need to understand the basic theory behind what is called transactional analysis. This is simply a method of understanding why you (or your teen) is reacting a certain way. Once you understand the reason behind your typical reaction, you can learn how to respond so you solve problems rather than cause them. Here's a short course that could revolutionize your interactions.

Every person is made up of three personalities. The first personality is called the CHILD, because that's the impulsive, irresponsible, emotional side of a person. It's the personality of inferiority. Anytime someone criticizes you or demeans you, you will tend to react in your CHILD, in an impulsive, irresponsible, or emotional way.

The second personality is called the PARENT, because that's the responsible, bossy, competent side. It's the personality of superiority that tends to make others feel inferior. If someone acts irresponsibly or without thinking, your tendency is to react in your PARENT personality, treating that person like a child.

The third personality is called the ADULT. It's the personality of equality. You don't say things to put the other down nor do you act irresponsibly when your ADULT is in control. People acting in their ADULT solve problems in a way that is mutually satisfying to all. This, of course, is the ideal relationship, one that gives the message that "I'm OK" and "You're OK, too." In fact, Thomas Harris' book *I'm OK, You're OK* should be required reading for both teenagers and their parents because once you know the lingo, this skill can become a game. Here's how the game can work:

If someone yells impulsively at you, you immediately recognize that he is acting as CHILD. You know that unless you consciously decide to react in your ADULT, you will slip into your PARENT and treat this person as he deserves to be treated, making things worse rather than solving the problem. So, as soon as you perceive his CHILD, simply say, "Your CHILD is showing!" When someone makes you feel inferior, just say, "Your PARENT is a little strong!" And if that person is into the game, that might be enough for him to refocus and respond in his ADULT.

Teenagers, especially, enjoy this game. And it can help remind parents to treat their almost grown-up child in a respectful, adultlike fashion. If only every word and action in the home could be monitored by the question, "Am I showing respect to others?" Showing respect is the best way to gain the self-respect we all desire.

And finally, the parent's most meaningful character-building task during these teenage years is to just be a good example. Live a Christlike life and be open and willing to share with youth the beauty of God's character and what God is doing in your life. Don't misunderstand. I don't mean to preach. Just live your beliefs radiantly, and joyfully share the experiences you have with the Lord. Let them bubble out—in your attitude and in your enthusiasm for living. When you live what you believe and are willing to give your child appropriate independence, you will keep a healthy, loving rapport with him, and your own loving nature will encourage him to establish his own positive identity. Idealistic? Yes, but ideals are like stars. You may never reach them, but you can set your course by them. Make this your goal throughout the growing years. Let your child see that your character comes from the inside out.

A PLAN FOR BUILDING CHARACTER

You now have a great deal of information on how to be an effective character builder. Only one thing is missing—a specific plan to use with your children. This plan must fit your family and your family's life-style. If you are the type that plans months in advance, you'll want to organize this program in the same way, but be accommodating—needs do change. If you enjoy scheduling a daily time when you present specific character-building information, you'll want to plan for this—but don't forget to be spontaneous. In other words, don't be so tied to your plan that you can't scape your ideas for the day and take advantage of a teachable moment. For example, if a TV special on world hunger has just aired, talk about social issues, justice, and the importance of reaching out to those in need, even though the topic of the day *might be orderliness!*

If you are the type of family that enjoys a more flexible program, you should develop a framework that works for you, making sure you teach your children these concepts in a more informal way as you interact throughout the day. Character building should not be a burden, otherwise you will resent the time you must spend at it. Remember, your character, which is reflected in your attitude and your behavior, will ultimately have a greater impact upon your child than any story or object lesson. Then why do you need a plan? Because a plan helps you focus on what you really want to teach your child—and how. The years slip away so quickly. With a plan, you won't neglect an important area of training, only to discover its omission when the critical window of opportunity has closed. It's like an insurance policy. You want to make your child has the proper coverage at the time he needs it!

You may want to consider the plan Benjamin Franklin used to systematically develop his character. He worked on thirteen character traits—one for each week of the quarter and then repeated these same virtues the following quarter. With this plan he emphasized a particular trait four times a year.

Franklin chose thirteen traits that were unique to his needs. Jan and I have used this plan. In appendix A, you will find the thirteen character traits that we selected to emphasize with our children during the preschool and early school years. As our children grew our plan changed to include virtues that were more applicable to older children, such as serving others, acceptance of cultural and racial differences, concern for national and international social issues, and a sense of personal mission. For the first quarter of your character-building program, you may choose to develop some of the same traits as we did, since most of the hard work of finding supporting material has already been done for you in appendix A. But as soon as possible, you will want to build your own program, because your children are unique and have different needs. You will want to choose those traits that you feel they need in order to develop strong, noble characters. If you follow the weekly plan, you will want to select a Bible text and a song to use throughout the week. The next quarter these may be repeated, or new ones can be selected. Then you must find stories, songs, activities, and other supporting material that will help to develop your chosen traits.

Developing your character-building plan is an ongoing process. As new songs, texts, and stories are found that are appropriate to each trait, write them down. Some families may find it more convenient to use a filing system to keep track of character-building material. Others may want to write their ideas directly on a calendar that is used specifically for this purpose.

Ask for God's guidance as you develop your plan. It's a human tendency to try to do things all by ourselves, especially if we have just read a "how-to" book. But, God has ways and means of helping us with this awesome character-building task, if we but do our best. Invite God's Spirit to work through you as you begin building your child's character—the most valuable treasure on earth.

The chapters in this section will guide

you through the designing process, so that by the end you will have developed a plan specifically suited for your children. God bless you as you prayerfully search for His purpose for your child's character development—from the inside out.

Chapter 18
SELECTING CHARACTER TRAITS

Proverbs 22:6 says that parents should "train up a child in the way he should go." The problem lies in our understanding of what that way is. You know what characteristics you would like your child to develop, but what is best for him? And what does God say about the way a child should go?

Step One: Determine Your Own Child's Needs

Each child is different. Yours is unique. There is not one person exactly like him in the whole world. A developmental psychology course presents the normal—that which occurs or is expected to occur in the majority of children. But all the psychology in the world won't help you be an effective character builder if you fail to study the personality, temperament, and behavior of your own child. You must know your child, so that you can make meaningful applications to your own situation.

Researchers have tried to lump children into categories. For example, there is the child who is fairly easy to get along with—who is quick to adapt, has a positive mood and regular body functions, is placid in responses and eager in new situations. Characteristics of a more difficult child are being extremely active, slow to adapt, negative in mood, irregular in body functions, highly intense in responses and inclined to withdraw from new situations. If children were neatly divided into these two categories, we could set guidelines for each. But rarely is a child 100 percent "easy" or 100 percent "difficult." Each child poses a special challenge for character builders.

Some characteristics may vary, depending on age and family situations. Others may be fairly stable from birth. Most characteristics are more easily molded in early childhood, but change is always possible. If not, there would be no need for a character-building plan!

Because children are so different, you must study each child to be able to determine the "way he should go." I have found that taking a course or reading a good book on normal child development can be extremely enlightening to parents. Of course, you can raise children without this scholarly knowledge by using your God-given common sense, but a study of children and their behavior can be a valuable asset.

With this background you can more easily determine whether an undesirable trait that you are observing in your child is just a natural phase that will pass in time or something that should be dealt with, perhaps even by a professional.

Masturbation, for example, often worries parents. But knowing about how a child's genital interest develops can help a parent know how to deal with this. Toddlers and preschoolers are naturally interested in their bodies. They will explore themselves, including their genitals. There is nothing wrong with an occasional bit of curiosity, but if it's not properly dealt with it can escalate to a more serious problem. That's what a knowledge of child development will give you—an understanding of what is normal and what is not, and suggestions for handling the problems of each stage.

Armed with an understanding of normal child development you are now ready to take a closer look at your own child. Sometimes parents live so close to the "problem" that they fail to recognize it as a problem, or they may exaggerate its importance. Here are some ways to get to know your child better. In the process, you will begin to get a clearer vision of the character traits you will want to emphasize in your plan.

1. Take time. Watch carefully. Does your three month old use his thumb and forefinger to pick up small objects? Does your one year old consistently reach for things with his left hand? Does your 2 1/2 year old say "that" or "dat"? What does your child pray about, dream about, or talk about when you're alone with him? You'll never know if you don't spend time with him.

2. Observe your child in various situations. Is the only time you see your child at home between the hours of 5:30 and 8:00 P.M. when he's hungry and tired? Have you observed him at school, at a birthday party, at church? Is his home behavior the same as elsewhere? If not, what can you learn by the difference?

3.   Look at specifics. Does your child whine a lot? Is he constantly into things? Does he frequently hit his little sister? Probably not, but you notice these things often enough to think it is constant. To find out just how bad a problem it is, count (for three days) the number of times the behavior occurs per day. Then when you begin to work on solving the problem, you will be able to tell if you've made any headway. Notice what leads up to the problem. Notice the look on your child's face. Notice his reaction to you. These specifics should give you clues on

how you can be more effective as you work with him.

4. Be objective. Most of us see our children as extensions of ourselves. This can be rewarding when we notice their good behavior, but discouraging when we notice the bad. This can also cause us to be ineffective disciplinarians. We may either pounce on behavior that rubs us the wrong way or ignore behavior that we have tended to ignore in ourselves. So, being aware that we have this tendency, we must exert extra effort toward being objective. We must view each child as an individual in his own right. We must even occasionally look at him through the eyes of a stranger. You may be amazed at what you learn from this "impersonal" glance!

After studying your child's needs, make a list of the character traits that you feel should be emphasized in your character-building plan. Then modify your list as you continue through the steps in this chapter.

Step Two: Consider Desirable and Undesirable Traits

What do you consider to be the most desirable traits for a child to have? List these. Next, list what you consider to be the least desirable traits for a child to have. Compare the two lists.

Most Desirable	Least Desirable
1. _____	1. _____
2 _____	2. _____
3. _____	3. _____
4. _____	4. _____
5. _____	5. _____
6. _____	6. _____

7. _____ 7. _____
8. _____ 8. _____
9. _____ 9. _____
10. _____ 10. _____
11. _____ 11. _____
12. _____ 12. _____
13. _____ 13. _____

Step Three: Consider How Character Traits Develop

Did you know there is a step-by-step guide to character development in the Bible? It is found in II Peter 1:5-7 (KJV) "Add to your faith virtue; and to virtue knowledge; And to knowledge temperance [self-control]; and to temperance patience [perseverance]; and to patience godliness; And to godliness brotherly kindness; and to brotherly kindness charity [love]."

Here's what *The Living Bible* says about this character-building plan:

Do you want more and more of God's kindness and peace? Then learn to know him better and better. For as you know him better, he will give you, through his great power, everything you need for living a truly good life: he even shares his own glory and his own goodness with us . . . his own character.

But to obtain these gifts, you need more than faith; you must also work hard to be good, and even that is not enough. For then you must learn to know God better and discover what he wants you to do. Next, learn to put aside your own desires so that you will become patient and godly, gladly letting God have his way with you. This will make possible the next step, which is for you to enjoy other people and to like them, and finally you will grow to love them deeply. The more you go on in this way, the more you will grow strong spiritually and become fruitful and useful to our Lord Jesus Christ. But anyone who fails to go after these additions to faith is blind indeed, or at least very shortsighted, and has forgotten that God delivered him from the old life of sin so that now he can live a strong, good life for the Lord.

So, dear brothers, work hard to prove that you really are among those God has called and chosen, and then you will never stumble or fall away. And God will open wide the gates of heaven for you to enter into the eternal kingdom of our Lord and Savior Jesus Christ.
(II Peter 1:2-11)

This is God's plan for character development, regardless of age. All of these traits are vital and all should be worked on by the developing Christian, but according to Peter, each step is based upon achieving the previous step. This certainly doesn't mean, however, that we shouldn't be working on another step even though we might be struggling with the bottom rung! These eight steps outline God's orderly sequence of development—a ladder to a more abundant life and to a more Christlike character.

As a student of development, I began to ask, "Could it be that these stages might be applied to the developing child?" Soon an interesting concept began to formalize. Erik Erikson had identified eight psychosocial stages of development. Along with other psychologists, he believed that people develop traits according to a certain pattern. Perhaps Peter was giving us a

Christian equivalent of a pattern of moral development. I listed the ages that Erikson had seen as key periods in development and beside them listed Peter's traits—his "ladder of life."

Age	*II Peter 1*
Stage 1: Birth-1	Faith
Stage 2: 1-3 years	Virtue
Stage 3: 4-5 years	Knowledge
Stage 4: 6-11 years	Temperance
Stage 5: 12-19 years	Patience
Stage 6: Dating, Marriage	Godliness
Stage 7: Parental period	Kindness
Stage 8: Maturity	Love

Now what does all this have to do with character? Could there be a developmental progression to Peter's list? Common sense tells me that just because temperance, patience, godliness, and kindness happen to fall at later ages, that does not mean that each attribute shouldn't be emphasized during early childhood, as well as later. But could it be that there is a developmental progression as to when one attribute should receive primary emphasis and could be expected to achieve a high level of development?

For example, could it be that after establishing, during that first year of the child's life, a sense of trust (or faith), we should place our emphasis on teaching the child virtues (certain rights and wrongs)? After all, this is what setting limits is all about. Then during the preschool years, our responsibility is to give him the knowledge and instruction he needs to make his own decisions. Based upon adequate knowledge, the school-age child is then able to choose to be temperate and to begin learning to control his wants and desires. Temperance does require a certain background of knowledge as to what to be temperate in and how to go about achieving success.

Patience is the next trait. Teenagers need to learn to control their impulsive criticism, emotions, and actions. Then they can grow in godliness. This results in showing real kindness to those around them and to those they live with. How better could this trait be developed than in the expanding family where parents give to each other and to their children? Finally, after a variety of life experiences, a person develops true maturity. Not until he can fully accept himself can he really love others to such an extent that he consistently shows the CRAFT components of love (Care, Respect, Acceptance, Forgiveness, and Trust) for all those with whom he comes in contact.

Perhaps this is the answer to true character development. But the eight traits mentioned in II Peter 1 do not comprise the only biblical list of important character traits. You will find more as you continue your search.

Step Four: Look to the Bible As a Guide

Before you make your final selection of traits for your character-building plan, go to the Bible for suggestions you might want to consider.

1. Review the characteristics of God as mentioned in Psalms 145–147. If our children are to develop characters patterned after God, we need to know what God is like. Write down those characteristics and what they mean.

2. Read about the fruit of the Spirit in Galatians 5:22, 23 and write them down.

3. Think about the list of positive traits given in Philippians 4:8. List them.

4. Consider those traits that Jesus called blessed in Matthew 5:3-12. What traits are mentioned and why are these important? If you have questions about what some of the terms mean, check a modern translation.

5. Read systematically through the Book of Proverbs. This is the best child-rearing guide we can find. What character traits are mentioned in this book? Jot them down.

6. Tackle the Book of Romans. Read the entire book so you can better explain to your children the important concept that they can't be Christlike by themselves—no matter how hard they try. They must daily learn to give Christ their hearts and accept Christ's new one. Then take a close look at Romans 12:9-21. Read these same verses from *The Living Bible*. It's really a beautiful description of inside-out character. Write down the traits of character mentioned.

Step Five: Select Traits Your Child Needs

Now your job is to carefully analyze all the important character traits you have been reading about and considering and choose the ones you feel are most important for your children at this time.

Think specifically about each of your children. Circle the traits listed below that you feel are important for their personal development. This list is not a comprehensive list. You may add other traits you consider important. If you have more than one child, write the child's name beside the trait.

If you follow the thirteen-week plan you will want to limit your final selection to thirteen. Remember your children's needs will continue to change. Therefore, periodically you will want to go back through the steps in this chapter and revise your plan. If your children are older, you might want to include them in the selection process. Character building is a family project.

accepting	*empathetic*	*modest*	*self-reliant*
adaptable	*enthusiastic*	*neat*	*self-restrained*
affectionate	*faithful*	*obedient*	*self-sacrificing*
appreciative	*flexible*	*optimistic*	*sensitive*
careful	*forgiving*	*orderly*	*submissive*
cheerful	*friendly*	*patient*	*sympathetic*
clean	*generous*	*peaceful*	*tender*
communicative	*gracious*	*persevering*	*thankful*
compassionate	*happy*	*poised*	*thorough*
conscientious	*helpful*	*polite*	*thoughtful*
confident	*honest*	*prayerful*	*thrifty*
considerate	*hopeful*	*prompt*	*tolerant*
content	*humble*	*refined*	*trusting*
courageous	*independent*	*respectful*	*understanding*
creative	*industrious*	*reverent*	*unselfish*
dependable	*joyful*	*satisfied*	*zealous*
disciplined	*kind*	*secure*	
efficient	*loving*	*self-controlled*	

ॐ

Chapter 19
TOOLS FOR BUILDING CHARACTER

Every craftsman in the trades has certain tools necessary for the success of a job. The plumber has a wrench; the dentist, a drill; the physician, a stethoscope; the artist, a brush. What are the tools necessary for building character? A degree in theology? An adequate income so that Mom doesn't need to work? The highest caliber school in the country?

No, I'm happy to say, these aren't the tools, because if this were so, very few of us would have much chance of being effective character builders. The answer instead is to make good use of the resources that you have. First, you have your own personality, interests, and skills. And, second, you can use music, object lessons, practical activities, books, and stories to teach important character traits. These are your basic tools.

Yourself

Your most unique character-building tool, and by far your best, is yourself—your personality, your interests, and the skills that God has helped you develop.

Enthusiasm is an important trait for our family. We love to be around enthusiastic, optimistic people. No matter how many stories we tell our children about how enthusiasm affects people, and no matter how many enthusiastic songs we might sing, how much will our children really learn if Dad is tired every time he comes home? If the kids can hardly get a hello out of him, much less a kiss? But instead, our life with Jan is sprinkled with a good bit of enthusiasm. "Hi, everybody! I'm home!" he shouts. "You won't believe what happened today!" Then he animatedly describes the situation in detail. "Kids, I have a surprise," he exclaims, as he unveils a fresh strawberry pie.

Now, I'm sure there are times when Jan comes home dead tired and doesn't feel very enthusiastic about greeting the kids or excited about fixing the malfunctioning toilet. What should he do? Grumble and gripe? That would hardly solve the problem. Taking the problem out on the family only magnifies it, and everybody ends up grumbling and griping. Jan knows himself and realizes that what he needs is a quiet time—resting, reading, or walking—before supper, and then he's back to his usual enthusiastic self.

It's important that we know ourselves well enough to realize that it is impossible for us to be happy, orderly, efficient, or peaceful all the time, even though we are trying to develop all these traits in our children and know we must be good examples.

Children would rather live with honest parents who are able to admit that they have failed, than with hypocritical ones who are unable to admit how things really are. For example, young married couples sometimes say, "My parents never had an open conflict in their lives. So the first time my spouse and I disagreed, I thought our marriage was falling apart. I wish my parents, instead of putting on a false front, had given us an example of how we could solve conflicts."

So, expressing one's feelings in words early in the game, before the feelings get out of hand, can be an educational experience for children. They see how the parent overcomes these feelings or solves the problem, and this model is much more instructive than presenting a false front.

You must guard against trying to act perfect and then blaming others when you are caught making a mistake. For example, what do I say when the children notice the speedometer registering sixty-five instead of fifty-five? Do I blame others? ("Everybody else is traveling this speed." Or perhaps, "If you kids had gotten ready quicker I wouldn't have to go this fast.") Or do I accept the responsibility for my error? ("I wasn't watching. Thanks for bringing it to my attention.")

How many bad points should we allow to be seen? Enough to show our children the process of problem solving. For example, if you're sad, your mood can affect the whole family. But it's okay to be sad as long as you are doing something about it. So try saying, "I feel sad, but I think I'd feel better if I could go for a walk. Anyone want to go?" Or sit down at the piano and play your feelings away. Or read a chapter or two from the Psalms. And then put the smile back on your face so your sadness doesn't affect everyone.

All the skills and abilities you have can become tools for character building. If you paint with oils, you can demonstrate perseverance. If you grow roses, you can teach the importance of faithfulness in watering and fertilizing. If you are a working mother, you can show your ability to get both jobs done by being efficient in the use of your time. If you are a photographer, you can explain the importance of orderliness in the darkroom.

Wow! What a resource person you are! After you select the character traits you want your children to develop, start listing how you, by being the person you are and by doing the things you are interested in, can teach your children the importance of developing these traits in their lives. Then use other resources, such as music, nature, object lessons, practical activities, and stories. You can be an effective character builder if you just use the tools of the trade.

Music

Even before birth a child can be influenced by the music his mother listens to. Classical and semiclassical music have a calming effect; rock, a stimulating one. Music can be an avenue to a child's soul at a very early age. The words of stories may not be meaningful to the six month old, but the sound of Mother's voice rhythmically singing will create an atmosphere of love, acceptance, and security—the substance out of which beautiful characters grow. How soon words become meaningful is difficult to say, but if the melodies and words that a child grows up hearing have a character-building message, they can become a meaningful reminder for life.

Parents need to supervise the type of music a child listens to during the years when Mom and Dad still have control. The sensuous, loud beat and offensive words of rock and heavy metal should be carefully monitored. The words are often pornographic and degrading. When your child is wanting the latest album, go with him to the record store and look at the jacket to see what message is portrayed. Read the words of the songs, if printed. If not, take time to listen to them with your child before purchasing the album. Jot down as many phrases as possible. Analyze the words to determine whether they have a wholesome message or not. Your child's mind is a computer with an automatic memory. Once something enters, it is there forever. One never knows what situation might trigger the recall of some questionable input. "Garbage in—garbage out" is meaningful lingo for computers—and for a child's brain.

When children have headsets, a parent cannot always be sure of the quality of music they are listening to. The peer pressure to be familiar with current rock groups and to know the top twenty is so great that many children listen to questionable music even though they don't particularly like it.

Christian music, especially hymns, will contribute to good character building. Look for those hymns in your church hymnal that you would like your children to learn. If possible, find hymns that have a message to reinforce a particular trait that you are teaching. Then make music a part of your character-building plan. Here are a few suggestions for making music time an unforgettable family experience.

1. Choose songs that are not only meaningful to your children now, but will be meaningful for a lifetime. The preschool years are not too early to begin singing songs that have weathered the test of time and will probably continue to be sung for decades. Of course, some hymns are more meaningful to children than others, so make the selection carefully. You may want to start with your own favorites.

2. Sing one verse (or the chorus) until it becomes familiar, then begin on the other verses.

3. Make sure your children understand the words, so that if you are singing "This Is My Father's World," they know that it talks about "the music from the spheres," not "the music from the Sears," which is a typical mistake of preschoolers today.

4. Illustrate the songs. A picture can be drawn for each new

hymn learned, or your children may enjoy illustrating the different things that are mentioned in a song, in either a series of pictures or in a mural. One hymn that my children have enjoyed illustrating is "All Things Bright and Beautiful."

5. Act out the words of the song as you are singing. Some children's songs are particularly suited for this, such as "Roll, Roll Your Burdens Away," or "Deep and Wide." But you can make up actions to other songs as well.

6. Encourage your children to accompany the family singing as early as possible, even if just with one finger on the piano keys, or with bells, pan lids or percussion sticks. An Autoharp is an excellent instrument for younger children to use to accompany the family, while older children may enjoy learning to play a ukulele or a guitar.

7. Sing the songs often. The more they are sung, the longer they will be remembered and the more meaningful they will become. Take advantage of the times you are riding in the car, washing the dishes, or hiking up a trail.

Object Lessons from Nature

How might an ugly toad with warts on his back help us to build beautiful characters? What about a lizard with a bright red head? Or a Mexican jumping bean?

God works in mysterious ways—and if we are willing to search, lessons of God's character can be found throughout nature—even in toads, lizards, and beans. (See, for example, James Tucker, *Windows on God's World* [Hagerstown, Md.: Review and Herald Publishing Association, 1975]).

The Holy Cross toad, who bloats himself with water during the rainy season and then burrows into the Australian desert, can store enough water to save the life of an aborigine lost on the dry, parched sands. The toad offers one drink of lifesaving water, but that's all. Christ offers us spiritual water that is essential for character development. The water He offers will never cease flowing (John 4:14).

The male Agama lizard of Africa has a bright red head, a brilliant blue-and-green body, a large number of "wives," and a broad territory. But in his quest to become greater, if he loses a battle, his wives will be captured, and he is banished from his territory. If this happens, he slowly loses his color and turns brown. If we set out to become the greatest, we may actually find ourselves the very lowest of all (see Matthew 18:1).

The Mexican jumping bean "jumps" because of a caterpillar inside the Mexican arrow plant pod. When the pod falls off the plant, the caterpillar will die if it stays in the hot sun, so it snaps its body against the inside of the shell until it "jumps" to a shady location. When the caterpillar becomes a moth and breaks out of the pod, it must feed and lay its eggs on the arrow plant. When the eggs hatch, the larvae again burrow into the pods to feed. In John 15:5 we are reminded that "without [Christ] you can do nothing." Just as the arrow plant is essential for the caterpillar's cycle of life to continue, so we must have Christ to survive.

Nature is filled with lessons that can help a young child understand more easily such things as God's mighty power (the same power that guides the stars and planets of the universe), the forces of evil (fire, floods, and weeds), the consequences of poor choices (young animals not staying hidden), the beauty of following God's plan (the lowly origin of the butterfly), and the reward of service (the stream giving water to the countryside).

Perhaps the principle that parents can best teach their children through nature is that when we live in harmony with the physical, mental, and moral laws of life, we can best experience God's blessings and a sense of well-being. But a decision to go against the laws of the universe brings discord, anarchy, and ruin. An example in nature might be the erosion that occurs when land cover is destroyed, or the destruction wrought by a raging forest fire set by a careless picnicker.

While reading about toads, lizards, beans, and the lessons they teach is good, reading is not as meaningful to young children as are firsthand experiences. When a child is able to cultivate the soil, touch a slimy worm, and taste succulent grapes, the lessons will be far more meaningful than mere book knowledge. Something unique happens to the soul when it is allowed to bathe in the beauty of nature.

As children become acquainted with the marvels of nature, they will become acquainted with nature's Creator, and the more they learn about God, the easier it will be to pattern their characters after the Divine. An excellent resource on character-building lessons from nature is *Character Sketches, Vols. 1, 2, 3* [Oak Brook, Ill.: Institute in Basic Youth Conflicts].

More Object Lessons
To get ideas for character-building object lessons, browse through some books at your local Christian bookstore. But don't be discouraged if the object lessons call for some chemical you have never heard of, or some materials that you don't happen to have on hand. To be effective, an object lesson doesn't have to be an elaborate production.

As you read the Bible, write down the beautiful lessons that are given, such as the sparrow falling or the numbering of our hairs, which remind us of how much God values us (Matthew 10:29-31). The good fruit that grows on the good tree reminds us of the positive effect we will have on others if we live a good life (Matthew 7:17).

The most effective use of object lessons is to make a lesson out of whatever you are doing, whether it is shelling peas, washing dishes, or pulling weeds. For example, when a child sees that a cut flower is wilting, you can explain that our lives are like that when we are cut off from God. When the ants get into the honey, you can mention that Satan makes sin seem so sweet that we are attracted to it, and if we are not careful, we can get stuck in it. When you are sponging off the table, squeeze the sponge out and then let the children watch how it soaks up the water. Explain that when our lives are empty, it is very easy to absorb whatever is around us—even the bad traits. But when we fill our lives with good things there won't be room for the bad.

Practical Activities

Building character is the work of a lifetime. And although it is important to delegate specific times for emphasizing the importance of various character traits, it is also important to weave character building into all family activities. Talk about moral dilemmas and issues. Discuss the pros and cons of various topics. Help your children to clarify their values by posing such questions as, "What would you do if you had a million dollars?" or "If you could just have one thing in the world what would it be?" or "What are the three things you feel are the thing is for parents not to insist on their own ideas, especially as children approach the teen years. And the children's ideas should not be scoffed at, no matter how strange they may seem. Keep an accepting and open atmosphere during family activity times, and you will be surprised at the impact this will have on your children.

As you develop your own character-building plan, you will want to schedule specific activities that will help your children develop certain traits. Some of these activities might be to write New Year's resolutions, to plan weekly Family Nights, or to bake cookies for a neighbor.

Through activities, the family can actually put into practice all those good traits that they have been telling stories about, learning Bible texts about, and singing about. The more children are encouraged to act out these traits, the more enjoyment they will gain from making others happy, and the more habitual these behaviors will become. The secret is not to hold all the goodness in, but to share it with others. This is the way noble characters are built.

Stories

We've already talked a lot about how stories can communicate truth about character traits. Children love stories. A healthy dose of the right kinds of stories can have a very positive effect on them. However, throughout the growing years you should be aware of what your child is reading. Here are some guidelines to help you select good character-building books:

1. Determine the message of the book or reading material. The book's entertainment value is not enough. Kids can have their appetite ruined for worthwhile reading material

by indulging in comics, romantic novels, and science fiction that emphasize worldly values. These can become addictive.

2. Is the writing interesting? Children tend to pick up books that are interesting to read. Take some time to explore the library and your local Christian bookstore. David C. Cook Publishing Co. has not only put their Chariot books in age-graded sequences, but has also identified the character-building trait or traits each book will help teach. Many Christian bookstores now feature this Chariot Children's Center, and it truly helps parents to use books as a character-building tool.

3. Not all good character-building books have to be Christian. The children's librarian in your public library should be able to point you to some good authors and storybooks that are appropriate for your child's age.

4. Be sure the books you get for your children are age-appropriate. Toddlers need a picture on every page with just a sentence or a few words. Preschoolers still need a picture on every page and enjoy real-life stories of people or animals. I've found that some of the best character-building stories for preschoolers picture animals with human characteristics. *The Way Mothers Are* by Mariam Schlein, the *Francis* stories by Russell Hoben, the *Little Bear and Edith* stories by Dare Wright, and the *Little Richard and Prickles* stories by Patricia Scarry were my preschooler's favorites.

School-age children still enjoy good illustrations, but not as many. For younger children big print and easily recognized words are important. If your child finds reading difficult, get the most interesting and the easiest books for him to read, regardless of his age. My boy enjoyed *The Picture Bible* up to his teen years because the pictures basically told the story. It was easy reading, and he was reading the Bible.

5. A child is never too old to be read to. For years, the bedtime ritual in the Kuzma house was to read a story or two from *Uncle Arthur's Bedtime Stories*, a wonderful set of character-building stories by Arthur Maxwell. We read all 10 volumes and re-read the kids' favorites again and again. When I started writing this book, I asked my teenagers what they felt had made the most meaningful impact on them during their childhood years, and they all mentioned different stories from Uncle Arthur.

    As my children graduated from preschool, I read to them the Laura Ingalls Wilder series and some Marguerite Henry books, such as *Misty of Chincotigue*, as well as some good biographies and stories written specifically for Christian young people.

    During those early school years I remember how much fun it was when they would get home from school and we would all cuddle up on our big bed as I read to the kids the next chapter of an exciting book. I don't exactly know when or why we dropped that habit. I guess extracurricular activities and homework weaseled their way into our lives. But now, as I look back, I really miss that time we spent reading together.

    One very busy working mom found that her kids didn't mind cleaning up the kitchen after supper if she read to them. They got through C. S. Lewis's *Chronicles of Narnia* and many other classics that way. Lewis's *Space Trilogy* (good science fiction) and J. R. R. Tolkien's *Hobbit* and *Lord of the Rings* sequence make great out-loud reading for older children. You should also not neglect the true classics, like *Little Women* by Louisa May Alcott or *The Secret Garden* by Frances Hodgson Burnett.

Stories of great people can be particularly meaningful to children. We found a large number of biographies, written especially for the school-age child, in the public library. One friend has read numerous stories to her daughters about Black heroines like Harriet Tubman and Sojourner Truth who worked the underground railroad in pre-Civil War days. Now she's reading them the short biographies in Great Negroes Past and Present. My children always enjoyed having us read from the Reader's Digest, Guideposts, and other journals about the lives of outstanding people.

6. Tell your children personal stories. The richest resource for stories comes from the lives of Mom and Dad, relatives, and the children themselves. "Daddy, tell us again about the time when you were a little boy and the train almost went off and left you." "Grandpa, remember that time you told us about the skunk? Tell us again." "Mommy, tell me again about when the dolphins swam around our boat and we were scared."

7. Make up character-building stories. For many years, my kids were entertained nightly by Jan's continuing "Wolfy" story. It was about this little "Wolfy," who was always get-

ting into trouble or dilemmas that closely resembled the happenings of the Kuzma kids. Many years later, as our kids were reminiscing about the "Wolfy" stories, Jan happened to mention that he made them up from household situations to teach them a character-building lesson. The kids were shocked! They had no idea of the hidden purpose behind the stories!

The stories you choose to tell or read to your children will have a lasting effect. That's why you must select the very best. The appendix carries a partial list of Christian books that can round out your character-development plan.

Chapter 20
THE GREATEST RESOURCE

Through the Bible we learn what God's character is like and how to have a saving relationship with Him, both of which are essential for developing inside-out character. As we learn more about God we can learn exactly what kind of character He wants for us and our children. This chapter will show you how you can use the Bible as a tool for building your child's character.

Using the Bible for Personal Study

God has provided the greatest character development resource of all in His Word. If you have not yet discovered how valuable this resource can be, follow these suggestions and I guarantee you'll gain new insight, will find yourself wanting to learn more, and at the same time will be a good example for your children.

First, choose the Bible translation with which you feel most comfortable. You'll enjoy your Bible study better and find helpful ideas more easily with one of the modern versions.

Second, have your goal clearly in mind. The primary goal should be to find the way that God would have children go. In other words, find the characteristics and behavior that are

Christlike. As you read you'll be surprised at how many ideas you'll get to help the children develop these characteristics. There are wonderful stories, parables, and object lessons just waiting to be found and used as you teach your children. Discovering these resources can be your secondary goal. Don't forget to pray for guidance. God knows best what you and your children need. Also, set aside a specific time to search your Bible for help (at least once a week).

It helps to search together. If Mom and Dad can become united in their quest, they will find that their approach in teaching Christlike characteristics and behavior will be more uniform. Another couple, with children of ages similar to yours, might enjoy studying with you.

Don't try to glean every idea at once. It is better to act on one small piece of information than to become discouraged with the enormity of the task. Read only as far as necesssary to get an idea that you feel is applicable to your child at this specific time.

You can keep a diary of your findings and your effectiveness. Write down the text and what it says to you. Also, write down what you are going to do about it. What changes are you going to make in your life because of your new insight into God's Word? How are you going to use this with your children? If possible, set a time when you will evaluate the effectiveness of your teaching—the responses of your children. Record your observations.

Be systematic. Choose one book of the Bible and continue reading it until you have gleaned what is applicable to you at this time. Or, if you are interested in specific character traits, stay with one topic until you feel satisfied.

Don't get discouraged. God has promised that "you will

seek Me and find Me, when you search for Me with all your heart" (Jeremiah 29:13). Christ, too, says, "Seek, and you will find" (Luke 11:9). Take God at His Word.

Finally, read Deuteronomy 5 and 6. Make a list of all the things this passage says that His people should do. Begin with the first verse. Listen carefully to all the laws God has given you, learn them, and be sure to obey them. Then consider what you should do. Specifically note Deuteronomy 6:5-7: You should love God with all your heart, soul, and strength. You should think about His commandments and teach them to your children. You should talk about God's law when you are at home or out for a walk, at bedtime and the first thing in the morning. This is your commission!

Bible Stories

Bible stories are a great way to introduce your child to God and to build character. Do you enjoy stories of conflict, high adventure, love, miracles? Yes, of course. We all do—and so do our children. Can you think of a more fascinating and intriguing tale than that of young David fighting Goliath? How would you like to spend three days in the belly of a whale or be fed by ravens? That's adventure! Our hearts are warmed by the love story of Solomon and the peasant girl or the bond of affection between David and Jonathan. When it comes to miracles, what greater are there than raising men from the dead or stilling the wind and waves? Mighty stories they all are—second to none that man in his most creative imagination can compose. And yet, each one is true—and each one reveals important aspects of the character of God. Plus, they are all found in one inexpensive, readily available book.

My friend Tim Hansel, President of Summit Expeditions,

tells a story about a kid coming home from church with a wild story about how the Israelites crossed the Red Sea. He said that Moses reached into his robe and took out his walkie-talkie and ordered the helicopters to put down a pontoon bridge. Then, after the Israelites crossed, he called out the jets and they bombed the bridge just before the Egyptians got there. When his mom asked if that was exactly the way his teacher had told him the story, he replied, "Well, not exactly, but if I told you the way she did, you would never believe it."

Why is it that such an intriguing book as the Bible gets so little attention in the lives of our children today? Are the stories too "far out" to be believable? Or do they reveal God's character in such a dramatic way that Satan is trying his best to cover their value in old English wording and delicate paper? Don't touch is often the first message that parents give to their children about the Bible. But when do they get the message, "Open and read—it's fantastic"? Are we, as parents, saying to our children, "Look what I found in my Bible this morning," or "Listen to this wonderful story I just read in God's book"?

There is more than one way of studying the Bible. At different times, in different places, and for different ages, Bible study should change. But for little children—and teenagers— there is no better way to inspire in them a love for God's mighty book than by opening the Bible and telling the stories in your own words, making applications to the things that are familiar and real in your children's lives.

Take the Jonah story for instance: Jan had his own version for our preschoolers. It went something like this: "And when Jonah went back to Nineveh he told the people they had better stop doing all the bad things that they were doing. They were not to eat candy between meals, they were to say their prayers and learn their memory verses, be kind to their brothers and sisters, obey their parents, and when they made mistakes they were to ask Jesus to forgive them."

Well, that's not exactly what Scripture says, but these are the things that have meaning for little children. This is what they can understand. It's these specific things that can help them become better people and build better characters, rather than something so abstract as the word "repent."

Our teens can be led into a deeper knowledge of God through Bible stories, too. Here's one I recently told my kids:

He loved her from the beginning. As youngsters, they used to play together in the sand under the pomegranate trees while their mothers washed at the well and exchanged tidbits of gossip and recipes. She was always laughing, flitting from one thing to another, flashing her dark, gypsy eyes at every passerby.

She was younger, like a little sister to Hosea. Maybe that's why he always felt responsible for her. She just seemed to court trouble. Like the time she said she'd kiss the boy who would bring her honey from the old tree stump, and she herself ended up being in the flight path of the angry wild bees. What if Hosea hadn't been around to rescue her?

You would have thought she would admire this older, sensible boy—her conscience and her guardian. But she didn't. She brushed him off as she would have a home-spun shawl that irritated her sensitive skin.

Their years as youth found them embarking on divergent paths. Hosea—responsible, stable, disciplined, turned toward God. Gomer—the beautiful, flirtatious tease, turned toward pleasure. Hosea had tried to warn her about her so-called friends, Jotham and Corbin, who had only one thing on their otherwise empty minds—the conquest of women. Hosea had overheard their boasts and their snide remarks about "easy prey," and then the challenge, "Go for Gomer!" But Gomer laughed at his over solicitousness and shook off his concern something like a dog might try to rid itself of an annoying flea. "Oh, Hosea, go back to your scrolls and your feasts. I can take care of myself!"

It hurt him to see her partying with the crowd from town and being led from the timbrel and lyre to the shadowy places away from the dancing. It took little imagination for Hosea to guess what Jotham, Corbin, or one of the others who were drunk from too much wine and impassioned by the beat of the sensual music, wanted from Gomer.

During the months that followed he saw very little of her. He had caught a glimpse of her once bedecked in an elegant, white linen gown and gold braiding in her hair.

"Probably gifts from some lover," he thought as he shook his head sadly. "If only . . ."

He was well into manhood now—tall, handsome, with bronzed muscles from long hours in the sun as he nurtured the date palm grove that he had inherited. Some would have considered him a man of means, with resources enough to justify the taking of a wife and certainly capable of providing more than the necessities for a growing family.

He, too, began to feel the inner stirring that a man in his maturity feels—the need for a wife, a companion, a lover.

Hosea, now, wise beyond years, went to his heavenly Father with a plea, "Find me a wife. One that will be a helpmate, a mother to my children, and a source of continuing joy."

And God said, "Take Gomer, the prostitute!"

"But, God, you've got to be kidding."

"You love her, don't you?" God replied.

"Yes, oh, you know how much I love her; I've loved her from childhood. But, Lord, I've resisted my human desire for her because her selfish and worldly life-style has brought me more sorrow than I thought I could bear.

"I have prayed for Gomer, wept for her, and pleaded with her, but she would not listen. She only has one thing on her mind—the pursuit of her own pleasure. Lord, as much as I love Gomer, I am wise enough to see that life with her would be only bitterness and heartache."

And the Lord answered, "Take Gomer as your wife. Love her as I have loved Israel. She will leave you. She will prostitute herself by chasing after other lovers. But you will buy her back, as I will redeem Israel. You, Hosea, and your life with Gomer, will be an object lesson to my people."

"But, Lord, what about me—what about my happiness?"

"You will find happiness, Hosea, not in Gomer—but in following My will."

And Hosea did as God commanded.

Then I asked the kids if they thought Hosea found happiness. I sent them into the Book of Hosea to discover the rest of the story. We talked about what they learned about God's love from Hosea's story—and the kind of love we should have for others.

Using a little imagination to fill in the background of a Bible story and making it more personal is a great way to have the Bible come alive. And it's not hard to do; even kids can do it. Get them involved in telling Bible stories. Ask each family member to tell the story from the perspective of one of the characters in the story. Not long ago our family did this with the story of Jesus on the shores of Galilee, healing the demoniac. The demons get into the herd of pigs and they fall over the cliff. Jan took the disciple Peter's viewpoint. Kevin took the part of children who just happened to be watching. Grandma was the wife of the demoniac, and I told the story as the owners of the herd of swine might have told it. Once you hear the story from these different perspectives, it will never be the same again. Suddenly you feel you were a part of it. You experience it, and that's exciting!

Here are some other ideas about how you can make the most of Bible stories in your character-building plan.

1. *Act out the stories.*

> As you tell a story, dramatize certain points. Have the children act out roles in familiar stories. Some families keep a box of Bible costumes (bright-colored cloth, belts, robes, jewelry, crowns, etc.) for this purpose. Props are also helpful. I'll never forget the time our children acted out Noah and the ark. They brought the canoe into the living room and marched all 158 of their stuffed animals into the ark.

> One evening for worship, Jan had given the girls the assignment to put on a play. Later they came out of their room with their Barbie dolls. "Girls, I told you to get something ready for worship, not to play with your

dolls," Jan said in disappointed voice.

"But, Daddy, we did get something ready for worship." They proceeded to set up their Barbie dolls (and a few Ken dolls) and acted out the entire Queen Esther story. It was beautifully done. So, why not use Barbie dolls, people puppets, or even faces on fingers to portray these stories in a meaningful way?

2. *Pantomime the stories.*

   Just acting out a Bible story without words can be a fun experience for children, especially when the family has to guess what the pantomime is about. It sends the whole family to the Bible—the kids trying to find a story no one will guess, and Mom and Dad trying to find the answer.

3. *Tell a parable.*

   The parables that Christ told are among the most meaningful stories ever told. Encourage family members to make up their own parables that illustrate a Bible truth.

4. *Illustrate stories.*

   Children are captivated by illustrations. Have you ever thought of illustrating your story? It doesn't have to be fancy. Stick people will be fine. Using a chalkboard and drawing as you talk might also be meaningful. The children can be encouraged to illustrate their favorite story.

Encourage Bible Study and Memorization

As children get older, they should be encouraged to open

the Word on their own and have personal devotions, rather than feel they must always be spoon-fed by Mom and Dad. Memory verse cards can be carried in their pockets. The importance of various character traits can be made clear by having them memorize Bible texts. Some examples: To illustrate happiness, quote "A merry heart does good like a medicine" (Proverbs 17:22). For honesty, repeat "Thou shalt not steal" (Exodus 20:15). For responsibility, "To obey is better than to make holy sacrifices" (I Samuel 15:22). For peacefulness, "Be still, and know that I am God" (Psalm 46:10).

So, when the kids are crying and you feel like telling them it's driving you crazy, tell them that you need the medicine that's given in Proverbs 17:22. The best way for children to commit Bible texts to memory is not only to learn them at a designated time, but to hear the texts used in practical ways throughout the day.

Memorizing the Bible is so important that we should make it simple and fun. Childhood is the easiest age to commit texts to memory. But children will rebel if made to "learn it, or else," or made to repeat it until they are "blue in the face." If a child has no idea what "dost" and "shalt" and all the big words mean, Bible memorization becomes a chore and whatever is learned is retained for only a short time. "Don't lie" makes much more sense to a preschooler than "Thou shalt not bear false witness."

Give your kids bite-size portions of Scripture to remember. Don't worry about memorizing a complete text if the important part is just a few words long. And don't criticize your child for getting some of the words or the word order wrong. Your goal is for him to commit to memory something that makes sense, even if it may not match the exact words of one particular version of the Bible.

Remember that you will have a great influence on how your child views Scripture. If you value it and use it daily (for instance, in everyday conversation), then he will, too. But if you use it as a hammer over his head, he will grow to despise it. In other words, after a child has taken a cookie that he shouldn't have, don't quote, "Thou shalt not steal."

Music can aid the memory. There are many scripture song books, or you can put a favorite verse to your own tune.

Choose texts for memorizing that are especially meaningful to your children—perhaps relevant to something happening in their lives at the time. And let them choose the texts themselves when they get old enough.

Your job as a character-building parent is to make the Bible so alive that your children are ready and eager to open it and read it as soon as they can. They should find the instruction and promises so helpful that they will be eager to commit God's words to memory. In order to make this happen, you should put your best thought and most creative efforts into teaching Bible truths to your children. Don't neglect this most important resource as you help your children develop spiritual character from the inside out.

*O*nce upon a time in the land of parenting, there lived two builders. Both had been given the responsibility to construct a building. Both had been given the counsel to start early. ("Train up a child in the way he should go, and when he is old, he will not depart from it." Proverbs 22:6) Both had been given the guidelines from the Master Designer. Both had been given the hot-line number where the Master Designer could be reached, with the instruction to stay in touch. And both had all the necessary tools to accomplish the task.

The first builder knew the responsibility was his, and he knew the counsel, but when he began reading the guidelines he said, "These instructions are too general. It is so difficult to relate these ancient guidelines to conditions today." And the more detailed plans seemed too idealistic. "It is impossible for me to build in such a manner because of the kind of world I

*live in and because of so many pressing respon-
sibilities. Besides, I want to know exactly how
hard and how many times I pound on the nail
to make it go in the right way, and these plans
aren't that specific. I don't have time to call the
Master Designer all the time. What will He
think if I bother Him with such little things?"
So he went his own way and built a little here
and a little there. He did this when his schedule permitted it, and when he felt like it. His
building grew, but it toppled in the storm.*

*The second builder took his responsibili-
ty to build more seriously. To understand clearly the Master Designer's counsel, he read the
guidelines from cover to cover, selecting those
principles that he could use to develop his own
set of plans that would meet his specific needs.
He studied the designs developed by other successful builders and rather than follow them
blindly, he searched for the architectural principles that would apply to his unique situation.*

*What a job! It would have been much
easier to follow blindly what others had done.
But in the guidelines of the Master*

Designer he found this challenge: "Look, the Lord your God has set the land before you; go up and possess it [build on it], as the Lord God of your fathers has spoken to you; do not fear or be discouraged." (Deuteronomy 1:21) And he took courage, picked up his tools, and began to build. He kept in constant contact with the Master Designer. He wasn't afraid to admit his lack of knowledge and to ask for help. He was thankful for the hot line!

He didn't do a perfect job, especially in the early days when he was new to the task. It takes time to learn. He pounded in a few bent nails. He even papered the wrong wall a time or two. But when this happened he said, "I'm sorry," and started again. Rather than hide his mistakes, he corrected them as soon as he became aware of them. Even though it took a little more time and patience, the results were worth it, for the building was nearly perfect.

After eighteen years of planning, pounding, papering, and polishing, the building, although not fully complete, was ready to stand on its own. And it did, through the wind and

the storm. When people came to the house-
warming they liked all of it from the inside out.

And the Master Designer said, "Well
done, good and faithful servant; you were faith-
ful over a few things, I will make you ruler
over many things. Enter into the joy of your
lord." (Matthew 25:21) And he did.

A SAMPLE PLAN
FOR DEVELOPING
CHARACTER TRAITS

My husband and I developed a character-building plan when our children were young. We used this resource for a number of years, modifying it to meet our children's changing needs. It was so easy to use that I decided it was time to share it with others.

We followed Benjamin Franklin's plan of emphasizing one trait a week for the thirteen weeks of a quarter, so each trait would be emphasized four times a year. The thirteen traits we selected were: faith/faithfulness, orderliness, self-discipline, happiness, perseverance, honesty, thoughtfulness, efficiency, responsibility/obedience, respect/courage, enthusiasm, humility, and peacefulness.

As you read the definitions we assigned to these traits you'll notice that they are broader than a dictionary definition might be. We deliberately did this so we could use this guide again and again, and each time emphasize a different aspect of the trait. For example, responsibility is an important trait, and so is obedience. But we put these two traits together in order to emphasize that our children's main responsibility was to be obedient.

For memorization purposes, you should use the version of

the Bible with which your family is most familiar, but the texts don't have to be memorized word for word to be meaningful. Simplify the texts for younger children. Many parents use an easier-to-read Bible such as *The Living Bible*. Even older children may benefit from putting the texts in their own words.

The texts we chose, as well as the Bible stories, are examples of both the positive aspect of the trait, as well as the negative. You may have to stretch your imagination to catch the significance of a few, because I don't explain why we made the choices we did. There are enough suggestions given so that you can choose the most meaningful for your family.

For the suggested songs, I chose a few familiar hymns that can be found in most hymnals. There are hundreds of children's songs that emphasize the different character traits, and they come from many sources. You'll want to collect age-appropriate songs for your family. Probably the most effective songs will be those that your child is learning at church. Reinforce the meaningfulness of these songs by singing them in your home and talking about their message.

The stories you use to support your character-building plan can come from many sources. One primary source is obviously the Bible. I've suggested a few of the most familiar Bible stories that illustrate the different traits. Read these stories for yourself and then tell them to your children, adapting them to your children's ages.

Another source are the books found in your Christian bookstore or church library. The publisher of this book, David C. Cook Publishing Co., has categorized all their children's books both by age appropriateness and by the character traits they will help you develop. See Appendix B for a list of books from Cook. One of the big questions parents often ask is, "Is this book right for my child." Therefore, any store or library which displays books by the age is a real resource for you.

Once you have selected the character traits you want to emphasize with your family, you will probably discover that you are looking for appropriate stories from many other sources—newspapers, magazines, and TV or radio reports. Make a note or clip the story and put it in a file folder. That way, when the week comes for the trait you have chosen, you will be able to use these easily.

I've also included a few character-related activities, just to give you an example of the types of things you might plan for your children. I did not give an extensive list, because activities are age-related. You will be the best judge of what is appropriate for your family.

What follows is a sample of the type of plan you can develop. I hope you will find this a helpful resource, although I did not intend that you use the sample plan exactly as we did. Be creative! A guide like this is always most effective when you make it fit the learner—and not the other way around.

Once you have a plan, you can creatively use these ideas throughout the day: telling a story on the way to school; singing a song as you fix supper; pointing out an object lesson as you play in the park; reciting memory texts as you and the kids jump rope. Building character is a full-time occupation.

FAITH/FAITHFULNESS

Definition: Complete trust (confidence or reliance); loyalty; allegiance to some person or thing; hope; unquestioning belief in God. Note that both aspects of faith are included—first to have faith, and second, to be faithful.

Bible Texts:

* *"Blessed is the man who makes the Lord his trust." Ps. 40:4*

* *"A faithful witness does not lie." Prov. 14:5*

* *"Trust in the Lord forever, for in . . . the Lord, is everlasting strength." Isa. 26:4*

* *"If you have faith as a mustard seed . . . nothing will be impossible for you." Matt. 17:20*

* *"Well done, good and faithful servant; you were faithful over a few things, I will make you ruler over many things. Enter into the joy of your lord." Matt. 25:21*

* *"Have faith in God." Mark 11:22*

* *"He who is faithful in what is least is faithful also in much: and he who is unjust in what is least is unjust also in much." Luke 16:10*

* *"But without faith it is impossible to please Him, for he who comes to God must believe that He is, and that He is a rewarder of those who diligently seek him." Heb. 11:6*

* *"Now this is the confidence that we have in Him, that if we ask anything according to His will, He hears us." I John 5:14*

Songs: "Faith of Our Fathers"; "He Leadeth Me"; "My Faith Looks Up to Thee"; "Anywhere with Jesus."

Bible Examples—Old Testament:

* *Eve showed lack of faith in disobeying God. (Gen. 3)*

* *Cain showed lack of faith by offering a fruit sacrifice. (Gen. 4)*

* *Noah faithfully built the ark even though he had never seen*

rain or a flood. (Gen. 6)

* The animals in the ark would have died if Noah had not faithfully cared for them. (Gen. 7, 8)

* Noah faithfully prayed to God the first thing after getting out of the ark. (Gen. 8)

* People built the tower of Babel because they didn't believe God's rainbow promise that there would never be another flood. (Gen. 11)

* Abram left home and family and traveled to Canaan because he believed God's promise. (Gen. 12)

* Abram showed lack of faith when he took Hagar as his wife so he could have a son, and when he told the King of Egypt that Sarai was his sister. (Gen. 12–14)

* God tested Abraham's faith by asking him to offer Isaac. (Gen. 22)

* Abraham's servant faithfully followed the instructions he was given for finding a wife for Isaac. (Gen. 24)

* It took faith for Moses to step into the Red Sea and then walk through it with walls of water on each side. (Exod. 14, 15)

* The Israelites lacked the faith needed to enter Canaan, so had to wander in the wilderness for forty years and die there. (Num. 13)

* Caleb and Joshua were the only spies who had faith that they could possess the land as God told them to do, so they were able to enter the land of Canaan. (Num. 13)

* Ruth left her family and country to be loyal to Naomi and God. (Ruth 1:16)

* Naaman was healed of leprosy because he had enough faith to dip seven times into the River Jordan. (II Kings 5)

* *Zedekiah ignored Jeremiah's advice to surrender to Babylon. (Jer. 38)*

* *Shadrach, Meshach, and Abednego were faithful to God and didn't bow to the image even though they knew they would be thrown into the fiery furnace. (Dan. 3)*

* *Daniel faithfully prayed three times every day even though he knew it meant that he would be thrown into the lion's den. (Dan. 6.)*

Bible Examples—New Testament:

* *Zacharias was made dumb (couldn't speak) when he didn't believe the angel who said that Elisabeth would have a baby. (Luke 1)*

* *Mary and Joseph believed the angel and fled to Egypt as they were told to do. (Matt. 2)*

* *The parable of the mustard seed illustrates how faith can increase. (Matt. 13)*

* *The disciples were afraid of the storm, but Jesus had faith that the wind and waves would obey His voice. (Matt. 14; Mark 4, 5; Luke 8)*

* *The woman was ill, but had faith that if she could only touch Jesus' garment, she would be healed. (Mark 5)*

* *The centurion had faith when he asked Christ to only say the word and his servant would be healed. (Matt. 8)*

* *Jesus walked on the water, but Peter sank because he put trust in self and not Christ. (Matt. 14; Mark 6, 7)*

* *Because Stephen was faithful, even to death, Paul was converted. (Acts 7)*

* *Paul and Silas were freed from prison by an earthquake but they faithfully stayed within the prison. Their faithfulness resulted in the jailer and his family being converted. (Acts 16)*

Activities:
* Show your children mustard seeds (or other seeds of a similar size) and talk about the importance of faith, even faith that is as small as a mustard seed. Plant some mustard seeds and watch them grow. Talk about how faith grows only if it is exercised (planted).
* List answers to the question: What should we have faith in?
* Have each member of the family suggest answers to the question: In what things should we be faithful?
* Make New Year's (or new week's) resolutions, and keep them faithfully.
* Talk about the importance of promises. Discuss specific promises that weren't kept and how that made the family members feel. (What effect does it have on the family when someone doesn't do what he promises to do?)
* Discuss the question: What is the difference between obedience, loyalty, and faithfulness?

ORDERLINESS

Definition: Regularity; neatness; tidiness; proper behavior; lawfulness.

Bible Texts:

✳ *"The heavens declare the glory of God; and the firmament [sky] shows His handiwork." Ps. 19:1*

✳ *"The law of the Lord is perfect." Ps. 19:7*

✳ *"He counts the number of the stars; He calls them all by name." Ps. 147:4*

✳ *"Let all things be done decently and in order." I Cor. 14:40*

Songs: "This is My Father's World"; "Lord, in the Morning"; "All Things Bright and Beautiful"; "Don't Forget the Sabbath."

Bible Examples—Old Testament:

✳ *The creation sequence was orderly. (Gen. 1)*

✳ *The specifications for building the wilderness sanctuary were followed perfectly. (Exod. 35–40)*

✳ *The camp of Israel was set up in orderly rows and by tribes on all four sides of the sanctuary. (Num. 2)*

✳ *Numbering Israel. (Num. 1–3)*

✳ *The priests were expected to conduct the sanctuary service in an orderly way. (Num. 4)*

✳ *The Israelites marched around Jericho in an orderly fashion. (Josh. 6)*

✳ *The book of the law had been lost because the temple was disorderly. But when Josiah found it, he tried to restore order to the kingdom. (II Kings 22:23)*

✳ *If the stars had not been orderly, then the wise men would have never noticed the special star that told about Jesus' birth. (Matt. 2)*

✳ *Jesus asked the disciples to pick up the pieces of bread and fish after feeding 5000. Everything was left orderly. (John 6)*

✳ *Jesus demonstrated orderliness when He carefully folded the grave clothes after His resurrection. (Luke 24)*

Activities:

✳ Make a chart to help your children to remember to do their regular duties, such as setting the table and brushing teeth, without a verbal reminder.

✳ Make a list of what needs to be organized in your home and make a plan to accomplish it (i.e., organize toy shelves, put game and puzzle pieces in correct boxes, clean out clothes closets and drawers, discard things that are too small or haven't been worn in a year).

✳ Organize the Book of Proverbs into categories.

SELF-DISCIPLINE

Definition: Temperance; self-control; moderation; patience; submission to authority; self-discipline is the result of orderly conduct.

Bible Texts:

✳ *"... choose for yourselves this day whom you will serve ... But as for me and my house, we will serve the Lord." Josh. 24:15*

✳ *"And everyone who competes for the prize is temperate in all things." I Cor. 9:25*

* *"For if a man does not know how to rule his own house, how will he take care of the church of God?" I Tim. 3:5*

* *"If anyone does not stumble in word, he is a perfect man, able also to bridle the whole body." James 3:2*

Song: "Dare to Be a Daniel"

Bible Examples—Old Testament:

* *Eve ate of the fruit from the tree of knowledge of good and evil when she knew she shouldn't. (Gen. 3)*

* *Esau was so hungry, he sold his birthright for a pot of soup. (Gen. 25)*

* *Samson's lack of self-discipline led him to marry a woman who destroyed him. (Judges 13–16)*

* *Joseph resisted Potiphar's wife. (Gen. 39)*

* *Moses' lack of self-discipline led him to kill the Egyptian, so he had to leave Egypt. (Exod. 2)*

* *Moses' lack of self-discipline led him to strike the rock twice instead of talking to it as God commanded. Water still came forth, but Moses was not permitted to go into the promised land. (Exod. 17)*

* *Daniel and his friends wouldn't eat the rich food at the king's table. (Dan. 1, 2)*

Bible Examples—New Testament:

* *Jesus fasted. (Matt. 26)*

* *Peter lost his temper and cut off Malchus's ear. (Matt. 26)*

* *John Mark "chickened out" (Acts 13:13) but later proved to*

be useful to Paul. (II Tim. 4:11)

Activities:
* Make a list of the things that each child feels he needs to work on in the area of self-discipline.
* Make a self-discipline chart and have the child put up stars if he did whatever was listed without being told.
* Talk about what the word "moderation" means.
* Have a "self-sacrifice" box for money that would have been spent on gum, sweets, or trinkets. Use the money for missions or for the poor.

HAPPINESS
Definition: Joy; contentment; merriment; cheerfulness.

Bible Texts:
* *"Happy is the man who finds wisdom, And the man who gains understanding." Prov. 3:13*
* *"A merry heart makes a cheerful countenance." Prov. 15:13*
* *". . . happy is he who keeps the law." Prov. 29:18*
* *"A merry heart does good, like medicine." Prov. 17:22*
* *"I know that there is nothing better for them than to rejoice, and to do good in their lives." Eccl. 3:12*
* *"A little leaven leavens the whole lump." Gal. 5:9*
* *"The Lord has done great things for us, Whereof we are glad." Ps. 126:3.*

Songs: "Lift Up the Trumpet"; "There Is Sunshine in My Soul"; "I Have the Joy, Joy, Joy, Joy Down in My Heart";

"Rejoice, Ye Pure in Heart."
Bible Examples—Old Testament:

* *Garden of Eden experience. (Gen. 2, 3)*

* *Jacob when he met Rachel. (Gen. 29)*

* *Children of Israel were unhappy in the wilderness. (Exod. 15)*

* *Hannah's joy when she had Samuel. (I Sam. 1)*

* *Solomon in his unsuccessful quest for happiness finally came to the realization that true happiness can only be found in living a life for God. (Eccl.)*

* *Ruth when she met Boaz. (Ruth 4)*

Bible Examples—New Testament:

* *Mary when she learned she would have the Christ Child. (Luke 1)*

* *Mary Magdalene when she discovered Christ was alive. (John 20)*

* *Paul and Silas when they sang in prison. (Acts 16)*

Activities:

* Put a drop of ink on a paper towel and watch how it spreads. Happiness spreads, too.
* Make bread out of yeast (leaven) and talk about how yeast grows.
* Practice wearing a smile all day, even if you don't feel like it.
* Sing as you work.
* Take a small gift to make a shut-in happy. Talk about how you felt after you did something kind for someone else.

* Discuss what the joy of Jesus was. (John 17:13)
* Discuss how you can be happy or joyful when bad things happen.
* Read Luke 6:22, 23. What should you do when people are mean to you? How can "leaping" or exercise help you feel better?

PERSEVERANCE

Definition: Continuing to do something in spite of difficulties or obstacles; steadfastness in purpose; endurance; diligence.

Bible Texts:

* *"Because of laziness the building decays; And through idleness of hands the house leaks." Eccl. 10:18*

* *"With men this is impossible, but with God all things are possible." Matt. 19:26*

* *"But he who endures to the end shall be saved." Matt. 24:13*

* *"Do not be overcome by evil, but overcome evil with good." Romans 12:21*

* *"... but one thing I do, forgetting those things which are behind and reaching forward to those things which are ahead, I press toward the goal for the prize of the upward call of God in Christ Jesus." Phil. 3:13, 14*

* *"... be strong in the grace that is in Christ Jesus ... endure hardship as a good soldier of Jesus Christ." II Tim. 2:1-3*

Songs: "I'm Pressing on the Upward Way"; "Work for the Night Is Coming"; "Onward, Christian Soldiers."

Bible Examples—Old Testament:

* *Noah continued to build the ark for 120 years. (Gen. 6)*

* *Ten times Moses went to Pharaoh to ask him to let the Israelites leave. (Exod. 7–11)*

* *Ruth gleaned long hours in the fields. (Ruth 2)*

* *Israelites continued to march around Jericho for seven times. (Josh. 6)*

* *Rebuilding the temple took persistence. (Ezra 3–6)*

* *Nehemiah persisted until the walls of Jerusalem were rebuilt. (Neh. 2–6)*

Bible Examples—New Testament:

* *The wise men did not give up following the star, even though their journey took many days and nights. (Matt. 2)*

* *The parable of the friend who came at midnight and received food because he persisted. (Luke 11)*

* *Parables of the one lost sheep (out of 100) and the one lost coin (out of 10) teach persistence until the lost is found. (Luke 15)*

Activities:

* Put a marble in an empty catsup bottle. Turn the bottle upside down and it will come out. Make the marble move around the sides of the bottle. If it moves fast enough it stays in, even when the bottle is upside down. Lesson: If the marble is idle, it falls out.

* Put a drinking glass between your mouth and a lighted

candle and blow. You cannot blow through the glass but the air flows around the glass (the obstacle) and unites on the other side and continues in the same direction, blowing out the candle. We must do the same with obstacles.

* Practice finishing what you start.

HONESTY

Definition: Truthfulness; integrity; fairness; sincerity; genuineness; purity.

Bible Texts:

* *"You shall not steal." Exod. 20:15*

* *"You shall not bear false witness against your neighbor." (You shall not lie.) Exod. 20:16*

* *"Even a child is known by his deeds, Whether what he does is pure and right." Prov. 20:11*

* *"Let us walk honestly, as in the day." Rom. 13:13, KJV*

* *"Do all things without murmuring and disputing, that you may become blameless and harmless, children of God without fault in the midst of a crooked and perverse generation, among whom you shine as lights in the world." Phil. 2:14, 15*

Song: "I Would Be True".

Bible Examples—Old Testament

* *Satan lied to Adam and Eve saying that they would not die. (Gen. 3)*

* *Rebekah and Jacob plotted against Isaac for the birthright. (Gen. 27)*

* *Achan was dishonest when he took a Babylonian garment, two hundred shekels of silver, and a wedge of gold, thus causing Israel to lose the battle of Ai. Achan and his whole family were killed because of his dishonesty. (Josh. 7)*

* *Joshua, against God's command, made a pact with the Hittites. (Josh. 8, 9)*

* *David was responsible for the death of Bathsheba's husband, but he tried to cover up his secret. His deception didn't work. (II Sam. 12)*

* *Naboth's vineyard was obtained in a dishonest way. (I Kings 21)*

* *The dishonest servant of Elijah got leprosy. (II Kings 5)*

* *Saul lied to Samuel when he said he had followed God's command to destroy everything of the Amalekites. (I Sam. 15)*

* *Eli's sons were dishonest in stealing from the temple offerings. (I Sam. 2)*

Bible Examples—New Testament

* *Herod asked the wise men to tell him where Jesus was so he could worship Him. This was a lie. (Matt. 2)*

* *John the Baptist honestly told about the evil thing Herod the King was doing, even though it led to his death. (Mark 6)*

* *Zacchaeus, the tax collector, was dishonest but repented and paid back those whom he had cheated. (Luke 19 and John 11)*

* *Christ told a parable about the dishonest servants of the vineyard. (Matt. 21)*

* *Judas betrayed Jesus. (Matt. 16)*

✳ *Peter denied Jesus and lied about who he was. (Matt. 26; Luke 22; John 18)*

✳ *Soldiers at the tomb accepted bribes and lied about the Resurrection. (Matt. 28)*

✳ *Ananias and Sapphira sold some land and told Peter they were giving all the money to him to distribute to the poor. They lied since they kept back some for themselves, and they immediately died. (Acts 5)*

Activities:
✳ Show a flashlight with bad and good batteries. Children may look the same on the outside but whether they shine in the world or not depends on what is inside (good battery).
✳ Twist a paper napkin into a tight rope. Pull to see how strong it is. Then put a couple of drops of ink or water (sin or dishonesty) in the middle and pull again. It breaks easily. This shows the effect of one dishonest act upon a person's character.

THOUGHTFULNESS

Definition: Consideration of others; kindness; compassion; gentleness; carefulness; attentiveness; heedfulness; thankfulness; love; reverence; courtesy; helpfulness.

Bible Texts:
✳ *"Oh, give thanks to the Lord, for He is good!" Ps. 107:1*
✳ *"Do not withhold good from those to whom it is due, When it is in the power of your hand to do so." Prov. 3:27*

✳ *"Cast your bread upon the waters, For you will find it after many days." Eccl. 11:1*

✳ *"... whatever you want men to do to you, do also to them ..." Matt. 7:12*

✳ *"... inasmuch as you did it to one of the least of these My brethren, you did it to Me." Matt. 25:40*

✳ *"... Love your enemies, do good to those who hate you." Luke 6:27*

✳ *"Be kindly affectionate to one another with brotherly love, in honor giving preference to one another." Rom. 12:10*

✳ *"And now abide faith, hope, love, these three; but the greatest of these is love." I Cor. 13:13*

Songs: "My Task"; "If Any Little Word of Mine"; "Rescue the Perishing."

Bible Examples—Old Testament:

✳ *Abraham entertained three strangers. He didn't know at first that one was Jesus. (Gen. 18)*

✳ *Joseph asked the butler in prison to remember him to Pharaoh. But he wasn't very thoughtful and it was a long time before he finally remembered. (Gen. 20)*

✳ *Rebekah was chosen to be Isaac's wife because she was so kind. She watered all ten camels of Abraham's servant. (Gen. 24)*

✳ *Rahab hid the spies, and her house was saved when the Israelites took Jericho. (Josh. 2)*

✳ *The servant girl of Naaman's wife thoughtfully told Naaman* that he should go to the prophet Elijah to be healed. (II Kings 5)

✳ Jonathan was thoughtful and loved David. (I Sam. 18)

✳ Abigail thoughtfully brought David food and later became his wife. (I Sam. 25)

✳ The widow of Zarephath unselfishly shared her last food with Elijah. (I Kings 17)

✳ Examples of thanksgiving: Priests (I Chron. 16:4; Neh. 12:31), Dedication of Solomon's temple (II Chron. 5:13, 14), David (Ps. 100:4; 116:17), Daniel (Dan. 2:23), Jonah (Jonah 2:9, 10), Jesus (Matt. 11:25; John 11:41), Anna (Luke 2:38), Leper (Luke 17:15, 16), Paul (Rom. 7:25; I Cor. 15:57).

Bible Examples—New Testament

✳ Jesus told the parable of the good Samaritan. (Luke 10)

✳ Jesus healed ten lepers, but only one said, "Thank you." (Luke 17)

✳ Jesus raised Lazarus from the dead. (John 11)

✳ Mary Magdalene poured perfume on Jesus' feet. (John 12)

✳ Dorcas made things for others. When she died Peter prayed and she was raised again. (Acts 9)

✳ Peter and John healed the man at the temple who asked them for money. (Acts 3)

✳ Epaphroditus visited Paul in a Roman jail. (Phil 4:18)

✳ Paul asked Philemon to be kind to Onesimus. (Philemon 10)

Activities:

* Children could do yard work (or other work) for an elderly or handicapped person.
* Write appreciation notes for kind deeds, or thank-you letters for gifts received.
* Plan a special surprise for some member of the family to show that you love them.
* Make a game of saying, "please" and "thank you," and of being polite.

EFFICIENCY

Definition: Ability to produce the desired effect with a minimum of effort, time, expense, or waste; working up to your capacity or capability; competency.

Bible Texts:

* *"Whatever your hand finds to do, do it with your might."* Eccl. 9:10

* *"And whatever you do, do it heartily, as to the Lord and not to men."* Col. 3:23

Song: "Work, for the Night Is Coming"

Bible Examples—Old Testament:

* *Joseph worked during the seven good years to save enough grain for the seven years of famine. (Gen. 42)*

* *When the time came to flee from Egypt, the Israelites had to flee quickly. (Exod. 13)*

* *God told Gideon to choose men who didn't stoop down to drink. (Judges 7)*

Bible Examples—New Testament

* *Jesus told the parable of the ten virgins which teaches that you must plan ahead in order to use time efficiently. The five foolish ones wasted their time going after more oil and didn't get to go into the marriage supper because they hadn't prepared in advance. (Matt. 25)*

* *Jesus told the parable of the unprofitable servant who buried his one talent. This teaches that God expects us to use what we have efficiently. (Matt. 25)*

Activities:

* Try to blow a candle out by blowing through a funnel, small end to lips. Then, blow through the big end and it concentrates the air to do the job.

* Put a piece of sodium, the size of a small pea, in a Pyrex dish half full of water. It will shoot back and forth spurting flame and smoke. It has lots of energy but does nothing worthwhile.

* Find ways to clean a room efficiently, like putting the block box near the scattered blocks instead of carrying each block to the box in the corner, or sorting clean clothes in various piles before folding.

* Pay a child more for jobs done quickly and thoroughly.

RESPONSIBILITY /OBEDIENCE

Definition: Obedience; trustworthiness; dependability; reliability; answerability; ability to distinguish between right and wrong, to think and act rationally, and to be accountable for your behavior.

Bible Texts:

✳ *"Honor your father and your mother, that your days may be long upon the land which the Lord your God is giving you."* Exod. 20:12

✳ *". . . to obey is better than sacrifice."* I Sam. 15:22

✳ *" 'Whom shall I send, And who will go for Us?' Then I said, 'Here am I! Send me.' "* Isa. 6:8

✳ *"I delight to do Your will, O my God, And Your law is within my heart."* Ps. 40:8

✳ *"Fear God and keep His commandments, for this is the whole duty of man."* Eccl. 12:13

✳ *"We ought to obey God rather than men."* Acts 5:29

✳ *"For to this end I also wrote, that I might put you to the test, whether you are obedient in all things."* II Cor. 2:9

✳ *"Children, obey your parents in the Lord, for this is right."* Eph. 6:1

Song: "Trust and Obey."

Bible Examples—Old Testament:

✳ *Eve disobeyed and wandered away from Adam in the Garden of Eden, after God told them to stay together. (Gen. 3)*

✳ *Miriam was sent to watch Baby Moses in the bulrushes. If she hadn't done her job she would have never known who found Moses, and he wouldn't have been able to live with his true family. (Exod. 1)*

✳ *God called Moses to go to Pharaoh. It was a big responsibility, and Moses was hesitant, but he finally went. (Exod. 3)*

✳ *Examples of mothers who were responsible and trained their children as God directed: Hannah with Samuel (I Sam. 2), Jochebed with Moses (Exod. 2), Elisabeth with John the Baptist (Luke 1), Mary with Jesus (Luke 2).*

✳ *If the Israelites failed to put blood on the doorpost the night of the Passover, the firstborn in the house was killed. (Exod. 12)*

✳ *The Israelites had to obey the instructions for gathering manna or they either went hungry or it spoiled. (Exod. 16)*

✳ *Gideon followed the angel's instructions. (Judges 6)*

✳ *Samson disobeyed and suffered the consequences. (Judges 13)*

✳ *Samuel had responsibilities as a child in the temple and answered God when He called. (I Sam. 2, 3)*

✳ *Absalom, David's son, was not trustworthy. (II Sam. 14,15, 18)*

✳ *David wanted to build the temple, but he yielded to God's will. (II Sam. 7)*

✳ *God told Elijah to tell King Ahab about the famine and then go find him after three years. It took courage to obey. (I Kings 17)*

✳ *Elijah's robe fell to Elisha, showing the transfer of responsibility. (I Kings 17)*

✳ *Josiah obeyed the law that he found. (II Kings 22, 23)*

✳ *Jonah tried to avoid doing what God asked him to do and ended up inside the great fish. (Jonah)*

Bible Examples—New Testament

✳ *The followers of Jesus went back to Jerusalem and prayed for the Holy Spirit as Jesus told them to do instead of rushing out and starting to preach as they probably wanted to do. (Acts 1)*

* *Peter and John went back to preaching in the temple after the angel helped them escape from prison. (Acts 5)*

* *Paul sent Onesimus, the slave who escaped, back to Philemon, his master. Onesimus went, even though he knew he could have been put to death for escaping. (Philemon)*

Activities:

* Talk about how we are like an envelope that goes where it is addressed to go. The Bible tells us where we are to go and what we are to do.

* Discuss how responsible people carry out their responsibilities. Next, make a list of the household duties of each family member. Be sure each agrees with this list. At the end of the week, hold a celebration to honor those fulfilling their responsibilities. Ask each person to help others by encouraging, reminding, and helping when necessary.

RESPECT/COURAGE

Definition: Feeling good about self and others; self-confidence; courage; treating others with honor, consideration, and courtesy. Note: our definition includes both respecting yourself as well as respecting others.

Bible Texts:

* *". . . for man looks at the outward appearance, but the Lord looks at the heart." I Sam. 16:7*

* *". . . Be strong and of good courage; do not be afraid, nor be dismayed, for the Lord your God is with you wherever you go." Joshua 1:9*

* *"You are the light of the world. A city that is set on a hill can-*

not be hidden. Nor do they light a lamp and put it under a basket, but on a lampstand, and it gives light to all who are in the house. Let your light so shine before men, that they may see your good works and glorify your Father in heaven." Matt. 5:14-16

* *"I can do all things through Christ who strengthens me." Phil. 4:13*

* *"Behold what manner of love the Father has bestowed on us, that we should be called children of God!" I John 3:1*

Song: "I'm a Child of the King."

Bible Examples—Old Testament:

* *Joseph in Potiphar's house respected God and himself enough to resist temptation. (Gen. 39)*

* *Samuel respected Eli by answering what he thought was Eli's call. (I Sam. 3)*

* *David, because he believed in God, had courage and self-confidence when he went to fight Goliath. (I Sam. 17)*

* *David showed respect for Saul when he wouldn't kill him. (I Sam. 24)*

* *Elijah stood before the whole nation of Israel at Mount Carmel and courageously spoke for God. (I Kings 18)*

* *Daniel, when captured, had enough self-respect to ask for a special diet. (Dan. 1)*

* *Daniel respected God enough to not be intimidated by the command to bow down to the king. (Dan. 6)*

Bible Examples—New Testament

* *If Jesus sees a sparrow fall, then we can be sure He sees and* *cares for us. That should make us feel valuable. (Matt. 10)*

* *Jesus did not embarrass Simon by announcing publicly the role Simon played in Mary's downfall, when Simon was unhappy about Mary's public demonstration of anointing Jesus. (Matt. 26)*

* *Mary showed her respect for Jesus by anointing His feet. (Matt. 26)*

* *Jesus showed respect to the woman caught in adultery when others accused her. (John 8)*

* *Paul had courage and self-respect when he went before King Agrippa. (Acts 26)*

Activities:
* Put six walnuts or pecans in the bottom of a glass jar. Add beans to the jar until it is half full. Shake the jar, and the nuts will come to the top. Explain that life is full of bumps, but the direction that we take will depend on our attitude. If we are "big" about problems, and don't complain, we will come to the top; if "small" we will go to the bottom with discouragement. Christ makes the difference.

* Have a stick which can easily be broken and a pipe the same length. Put the stick in the pipe and let the children try to break the stick. Point out that Christ will strengthen us if we ask Him, or if we are "hidden" in Him.

* Put a small candle on a small piece of wood. Float the wood with the lighted candle in a dish containing half an inch of water. Put a glass over the candle, and resting on the bottom of the dish. The candle goes out after it has used up the available oxygen (Bible study and prayer), and the water (bad habits) rushes in to take the oxygen's place. If

we want to shine in the world we need the oxygen of Bible study and prayer. Christ gives us the courage to be the example we should be.

ENTHUSIASM

Definition: Intense or eager interest; inspiration; zeal; fervency; ardor; optimism.

Bible Texts:

* *"Make a joyful noise unto the Lord." Ps. 100:1*

* *"Whatever your hand finds to do, do it with your might." Eccl. 9:10*

* *"If a person lives to be very old, let him rejoice in every day of life." Eccl. 11:8 (TLB)*

* *"Young man, it's wonderful to be young! Enjoy every minute of it!" Eccl. 11:9 (TLB)*

* *"[Be] fervent in spirit, serving the Lord." Romans 12:11*

* *"Rejoice in the Lord always. Again I will say, rejoice!" Phil. 4:4*

Songs: "Holy, Holy, Holy"; "Bringing in the Sheaves"; "For All the Saints."

Bible Examples—Old Testament:

* *David danced as the ark was brought into Jerusalem. (II Sam. 6)*

* *Elijah zealously prayed to God on Mount Carmel. (I Kings 18)*

Bible Examples—New Testament

* *John the Baptist was so enthusiastic in telling others about Christ that large crowds came to hear him. (Mark 1)*

* *Disciples preached enthusiastically after Pentecost and won thousands to Christ. (Acts 2)*

* *Paul was zealous in preaching on his missionary journeys. (Acts 16)*

* *Paul preached ardently on Mars' Hill. (Acts 17)*

Activities:

* Put liquid soap in a pan of water and slowly, lazily stir. Notice the difference when you stir vigorously and enthusiastically. Things happen.

* Experiment with various household tasks, doing them in a lazy, halfhearted way, and then with enthusiasm. Ask the children which they enjoyed more.

HUMILITY

Definition: Absence of pride or self-assertion; modesty; meekness.

Bible Texts:

* *"A haughty look, a proud heart . . . are sin." Prov. 21:4*

* *"Blessed are the meek, For they shall inherit the earth." Matt. 5:5*

* *" . . . everyone who exalts himself will be abased, and he who humbles himself will be exalted." Luke 18:14*

* *"He must increase, but I must decrease." John 3:30*

* *"Be of the same mind toward one another. Do not set your* *mind on high things, but associate with the humble. Do not be wise in your own opinion." Romans 12:16*

Songs: "Not I, but Christ"; "Father, Lead Me Day by Day"; "Live Out Thy Life Within Me."

Bible Examples—Old Testament:

* *Joseph proudly told his brothers about his dreams and that made them angry. (Gen. 37)*
* *Joseph interpreted Phaorah's dream and gave God the credit. (Gen. 41)*
* *Saul ceased to be humble when he became king. (I Sam. 10:13-15)*

Bible Examples—New Testament

* *John the Baptist, when seeing Christ, said that he (John) was unworthy and that Christ should baptize him. (Matt. 3)*
* *John the Baptist's disciples quarreled about who was greatest and John replied that Christ must increase, but he (John) must decrease. (John 3)*
* *There was a great contrast between the Pharisee's and the publican's praying. (Luke 18)*
* *James and John wanted to sit next to Christ in His Kingdom, and Jesus replied that whoever wanted to be first, must be willing to be last and to be a servant to all. (Mark 9)*
* *Jesus was humble enough to wash the disciples' feet. (John 13)*
* *The widow humbly gave all she had. (Matt. 22; Luke 20)*

Activities:
* Roleplay situations where a child is bragging. Ask the children to think of different possible ways to react and discuss the possible consequences.
* Help the children to notice and express appreciation when others do things well.

PEACEFULNESS
Definition: Freedom from disagreement or quarrels; harmony; cooperation; serenity; calmness; contentment; quietness; tranquillity; silence; absence of mental conflict.

Bible Texts:
* *"Be still, and know that I am God." Ps. 46:10*
* *"A soft answer turns away wrath, But a harsh word stirs up anger." Prov. 15:1*
* *"You will keep him in perfect peace, Whose mind is stayed on You." Isa. 26:3*
* *"Blessed are the peacemakers, For they shall be called sons of God." Matt. 5:9*
* *"Love your enemies, do good to those who hate you, bless those who curse you, and pray for those who spitefully use you. To him who strikes you on the one cheek, offer the other also . . ." Luke 6:27-29*
* *"If it is possible, as much as depends on you, live peaceably with all men." Romans 12:18*
* *"Do not be overcome by evil, but overcome evil with good." Romans 12:21*

Songs: "Peace, Perfect Peace"; "There Is a Place of Quiet Rest"; "When Peace, Like a River"; "Abide with Me"; "Be Silent, Be Silent."

Bible Examples—Old Testament:

✳ *Jacob and Esau were peacefully reunited. (Gen. 33)*

✳ *Moses killed the Egyptian and had to flee (broke peace) (Exod. 2)*

✳ *David played his harp for Saul to try to bring him peace. (I Sam. 16)*

✳ *God spoke to Elijah in a small voice—in a peaceful way, instead of in the wind or thunder. (I Kings 19)*

✳ *God promised Israel peace if they would obey Him. (Deut. 30:16)*

✳ *When the Israelites did as God commanded and destroyed their idols there was peace in the land. (Judges 10:16-18; 11:32, 33)*

Bible Examples—New Testament

✳ *Jesus was peacefully sleeping in the storm because He trusted God. (Matt. 8)*

✳ *Jesus drove the money changers out of the temple so it could be peaceful. (Matt. 21)*

Activities:

✳ Have two people play a duet on a musical instrument, but have one player start a few notes before the other. Comment on the discord and then enjoy the harmony when the players play the song together.